BRANDING IN A
DIGITAL
WORLD

HOW TO TAKE AN INTEGRATED MARKETING APPROACH TO BUILDING A BUSINESS

HILARY JM TOPPER, MPA

BRANDING IN A DIGITAL WORLD
HOW TO TAKE AN INTEGRATED MARKETING
APPROACH TO BUILDING A BUSINESS

iUniverse books may be ordered through booksellers or by contacting:

iUniverse
1663 Liberty Drive
Bloomington, IN 47403
www.iuniverse.com
844-349-9409

Because of the dynamic nature of the Internet, any web addresses or
links contained in this book may have changed since publication and
may no longer be valid. The views expressed in this work are solely those
of the author and do not necessarily reflect the views of the publisher,
and the publisher hereby disclaims any responsibility for them.

Any people depicted in stock imagery provided by Getty Images are
models, and such images are being used for illustrative purposes only.
Certain stock imagery © Getty Images.

ISBN: 978-1-5320-8749-3 (sc)
ISBN: 978-1-5320-8748-6 (hc)
ISBN: 978-1-5320-8747-9 (e)

Print information available on the last page.

iUniverse rev. date: 09/20/2023

This book is dedicated in memory of my mother, Phyllis Mass, and my sister, Lori Weiss, who were my biggest cheerleaders.

I also dedicate this book to my family and my online and offline community.

CONTENTS

PREFACE

It's been a decade since I wrote my first social media book, ***Everything You Ever Wanted to Know About Social Media, but were afraid to ask... Building Your Business Using Consumer Generated Media.***[1] After it was published in 2009, people bombarded me with emails and messages, telling me that social media would never catch on. I insisted that it was a viable option for marketing one's product or service.

👍 #TB

In November 2006, Lisa Gordon, my executive vice president, and I attended a Critical Issues Forum in New York City for the Council of Public Relations Firms. The discussion focused on X, Blogging, Content Creation, Facebook, Podcasts, and more. I left the event shaking my head.

"How could this take off?" I thought.

About a month later, my son decided to put me on Facebook as a joke to get his older sister angry. My first friends were Marcelle Fischler of the ***New York Times***, Jamie Herzlich of ***Newsday*** and Adina Genn of ***Long Island Business News***.

That's when I realized that social media was much bigger than I initially thought. I read all the books I could on the subject and followed key bloggers to learn as much as possible and realized that there was a knowledge gap. I wrote my first book to help educate people on social media. The book was ahead of its time. Many companies didn't buy into the fact that consumers were generating content and were the essential target market.

The world has changed in the past 10 years. Social media is so ubiquitous that if you don't have it, you are missing out on market share. New mobile apps come out every day to enhance the quality of life. Wearable technology is mainstream. Today, companies are even incorporating Augmented Reality (AR) and Virtual Reality (VR) in their marketing plans. Influencer marketing has become more significant than ever.

Therefore, it's imperative to create an integrated marketing plan for your brand that incorporates brand positioning, public relations, social media marketing, direct mail, email marketing and digital advertising to make sure your message is seen in your specific target market. In today's digital world, branding is paramount and being consistent with your image and messaging are of utmost importance.

In this book, **Branding in a Digital World**, I hope to help you learn to better market your product or service so that you can gain a competitive edge.

☝ What Makes Me a PR/Branding Expert?

Many people ask me how I decided to get into public relations and social media, and I say to them, "Do you have time for a story?"

In December 1979, I attended Long Beach High School. Long Beach is a barrier island off the south shore of Long Island in New York. My friends and I saw an article in the *New York Post* that was intriguing. Woody Allen was hosting a New Year's Eve Party at the Harkness House in New York City. My friend, Brian (who is now my husband), and my other friend made an appointment to tour the Harkness House for an upcoming event. We then took a ride on the Long Island Railroad to Manhattan and met with a manager at the Harkness House. The manager proceeded to give us a tour. We told him we were organizing a surprise party for my parent's 25th wedding anniversary. He thought nothing of it that we were only 18 years old, yet seemed to have the wherewithal to book a party.

To make a long story short, we drew up a schematic of the entire place, knew the location of the kitchen and showers. That New Year's, on the cusp of 1980, we dressed as caterers wearing black and white for Donald Bruce White (the official caterer). We hid our clothing under our trays and walked our way into the building. As soon as we had the chance, we ran downstairs to the shower room and waited for hours until the party started. We sat in the dark in silence. We heard nothing but the rumbling of trays and food preparation.

At around 9 p.m., we heard the party. We quickly changed and walked back upstairs like we owned the place. At the party, we met and mingled with the finest actors of the day – Robin Williams, Liza Minelli, Karen Kane, and Mia Farrow. Name an actor, and he or she was probably in that room with us.

We ate caviar and drank champagne. At the stroke of midnight, we celebrated with the rest of the actors and cheered! A few moments later, we made our way down the stairs and thanked Woody Allen for the invite. He looked confused. I even kissed him on the cheek!

When we got back to Brian's apartment (he lived in the Village at the time and went to NYU), I called the *New York Post* and told them what we did. They ran the story called, "Teens Crash Woody's Bash." I also called all of the newspapers and magazines and told them what we did. *Newsday*, WLIR radio and some of the local papers picked up the story.

Going from complete nerds in high school to instant celebrities was a fantastic thing. Overnight, we were branded the "cool kids." I said to myself, if I can publicize myself, I can do this for others, and that's how I became a publicist.

I've been a public relations practitioner for more than 30 years. I started my career as an intern at Public I Publicity in New York City, where I worked with entertainment clients. The following year, I worked at Clairol, Inc., in the PR department and interned at Ogilvy & Mather PR/NY. After graduating from Hunter College in 1984, both firms offered me jobs. I decided to take the Ogilvy & Mather PR position. There, I worked on many different accounts, including Dove Beauty Bar and Kinder-Care Learning Centers. When Hill, Holliday, Connors, Cosmopolous/PR opened its New York office, the CEO asked my boss and me to start up the firm's public relations department.

After that stint, I decided to try something different that would allow me to give back to the community. I landed a job at Altro Health and Rehabilitation Services and worked there for many years. Altro was a non-profit organization dedicated to helping people with psychiatric disabilities get job training and job placement. I started as the coordinator of public relations and later became director of public relations and development. The year that Altro merged with Federated Employment and Guidance Services (FEGS), I decided to go back into the private sector. I landed a job at Ruder Finn/PR and worked on the Jell-O, GLAD Wrap and Bags and other consumer product accounts.

I was drawn back into the non-profit sector when a friend, who I had worked with at Altro, told me about another opportunity in Queens. I decided to accept the offer, and became the public relations/development director at PSCH, Professional Service Centers for the Handicapped. The agency helped people with developmental disabilities and placed them in group homes.

About a year later, I became pregnant with my daughter and determined that the time was right to start HJMT Public Relations, Inc. I started the firm in March 1992 with a phone and computer. I slowly built up my client base and eventually moved the family out of an apartment into a house, where we converted the garage into an office. Several years later, I had seven HJMT employees working in my house. So, we decided to move to a suite in Long Beach, New York.

When the five-year lease was up for renewal, my staff and I strategically decided to move to Westbury, which was more centrally located on Long Island. By doing so, we tripled in staff and tripled in revenue. HJMT then made a move to

Melville, right off of the Route 110 business corridor, in August 2011. Recently, we made a full circle back to Long Beach and it is more vibrant now with the layers of knowledge and expertise we have cultivated through the years.

Today, we represent large businesses, small companies, and non-profit organizations by helping them with publicity, social media, SEO, website development, brand management, marketing, and graphic design.

In the following chapters, we will discuss how to brand your business using an integrated marketing approach. We will also discuss tactics to include in the plan like social networking sites, wearable technology, and the Internet of Things (IoT). Opinions stated in this book are either mine or from my online community.

I hope you get a lot out of this book, and my door is always open for questions. You can email me at hilary@hjmt.com, look for me on Instagram at @hilarytopper, friend me on all the social media sites mentioned in this book at Hilary Topper and you can follow me on X @Hilary25.

WHERE HAVE WE BEEN?

"*For professional communicators, the changes that technology has brought are both a godsend and an imposition. We can send messages to our audiences and contacts at lightning speed with efficiencies and targeting like never before. However, we're compelled to react so quickly; we leave little time to deliberate, plan, and fact-check. Subsequently, the victims of all these hyper-messaging are contemplation and accuracy.*" Jeffrey S. Morosoff, Chair, Department of Journalism, Media Studies, and Public Relations, Hofstra University, Hempstead, NY

When I started my career, branding was simple. Companies would take out advertisements in the newspapers and on television. As a result, consumers would buy their products. Today, due to the lightning speed of technology, branding and marketing one's product or services has dramatically evolved.

Before we can move forward, it's important to take a look back…

Close your eyes and think back to when you were young. Do you remember what technology you had in your house?

If you're a Millennial or a GenZ'er, you may remember always having computers, or, at the very least having a Gameboy.

Growing up, I had a black and white television in my parent's bedroom with no remote control and a single telephone that we kept in the kitchen. As technology became more affordable, I remember my parents buying a color television set. We were the first in the neighborhood to have a color set, and my friends were so jealous.

After that, we started to have phones in all of the rooms in our home, and eventually, my parents offered my older sister, Lori, her own phone number. That was a big deal. Everyone wanted his or her own phone line, Lori included.

My parents had a Super 8 camera that recorded on film that we played back on a movie projector. I remember sitting in the living room watching the movies we made, on a roll-up screen.

In the 1970s, the Polaroid Land camera was the next big breakthrough in technology. It was amazing because it had a film that developed within seconds. (Fanning the photos was half the fun!) Everyone wanted one. It was the hottest product around because of the sleek television commercials that enticed the buyer to want one.

We also had a record player that played 45s, 78s and regular LPs. My friends and I compared albums while listening to music. Lori was a big music listener too. My fondest memory was when Lori played her favorite songs over and over again, to learn the words. She favored Earth, Wind and Fire, Carole King, and America. I liked the more massive sound of The Who, Rolling Stones, and Peter Frampton. It's funny, recently, my younger brother, Ed, commented that he remembers me listening to music over and over again.

Before I graduated high school, the first Sony Walkman appeared on the market. Sony first introduced the Walkman as the "Soundabout."[2] Once they changed the name and refined their branding strategy, Sony expected to sell 30,000 of them. Instead, Sony sold 400 million. People listened to music through headphones and loved the portability of the product. My friends and I snuck our Walkmans into high school, but couldn't listen until we were outside, during recess or lunch, out of the teacher's sight.

When I went to college and lived in New York City, the Discman was the music device of choice. It was unbelievable! Compact disks fit into tiny little players, and we played our favorite CD while wandering through town. I walked around New York City listening to "Talking Heads 77." I played it over and over again because I only brought along one CD.

In the mid-1980s, when I was working at Ogilvy & Mather PR, we had a telex machine that allowed us to send documents internationally. This machine was so big that it needed a room of its own. Each desk had an IBM typewriter with correction ribbon, and if you made a typo, all you had to do was press the backspace key on your keyboard to erase it. For massive changes, you used liquid white-out or strips of white-out and would type over it after it dried. I remember working until 11 pm trying to make sure that every line and every word looked as perfect as possible and that the white-out did its job.

A few months into my first job, management announced that everyone in the organization was getting a word processor. I remember the other assistant account executives getting upset. I was angry too.

"If we learn word processing, then we will never be able to move up," my friend Sheila told me, upset that we would be forever stuck in our current positions when we were capable of so much more.

"I worked too hard in college to be a secretary for the rest of my life," said my friend Nancy.

Of course, that wasn't the case. Having a word processor made it so much easier to edit. Instead of staying until 11 pm, we finished our work by 9:30 pm. (Such is life at a public relations agency!)

I even remember the first Macintosh computer. It was so incredibly cool. It was a small little box-shaped machine that sat on your desk. It had a graphic user interface complete with smiley Mac and dogcow (that made "moof" sounds). The Mac could do so much, and you didn't even need to know primary computer language to use it. Shortly after that, computers became ubiquitous. Businesses had computers, and so did families. Computers became smaller and more compact.

In the 1980s, my husband, Brian, worked at Westlaw, a provider of legal research services. He trained other attorneys on the Westlaw system and conducted legal research. I was amazed at all of the information at his fingertips. He could find out so much with the click of a few buttons. Back then,

I never realized that technology would continue expanding at such a rapid pace.

In the late 1980s early 1990s, mobile phones came onto the market. At first, you only saw them in people's cars. My father-in-law was one of the first to have one. Then you saw people with them on the streets. Those who were chatting on phones while walking looked as if they held a loaf of bread to their ear! My friends and I thought those calls must be critical.

"Why wouldn't someone wait until they got to a payphone to make a call?" we asked each other.

Today, there are very few, if any payphones around. Now, if you don't have a smartphone, people look at you strangely. Smartphones have become the primary number, and many people have given up on their landlines because of excessive, unwanted solicitation calls, and also because they don't want to pay for two lines.

Within the past ten years, the trend has been to send a text message, that is, a short message service or SMS, instead of talking.

In March 1992, when I started HJMT Public Relations, Inc., my public relations and social media agency, out of my one-bedroom apartment in Long Beach, I had a rotary telephone and an Apple computer. That was all I needed.

Today, all you need is a smartphone and possibly a laptop. One important change is that now we also communicate via social networking sites. Every day, I talk with my friends, clients, and business associates on Facebook. That's how I stay connected.

In addition to communicating via emails and instant messages, I also use FaceTime to talk live to people. Alternatively, I use Zoom.us to feel connected to my community because I get to see them through the computer camera.

Most times, it all seems too distracting. Yet, if you think back to simpler eras, our communication method was just as distracting. You would be in the middle of some task and the phone or doorbell would ring. Times are changing and we need to change with them to find that perfect balance in our lives as technology continues to evolve.

According to Hootsuite,[3] more than 4.62 billion of the world's population is using social networking sites. With those numbers so high, it's important to learn to brand yourself through social media. Influencers, brand marketers and even small business owners have reaped the benefits of using an online strategy to build their brands.

☝ **My Observation...**

Technology has changed the way public relations practitioners position their clients. Brands need to be aware how to best reach consumers in this digital world. The future is unknown as to what technology will come but one thing is for certain, we need to be open to new ways to target consumers.

WHO

WHO ARE YOU? YOUR PERSONAL BRAND...

"All of the leaders I know who have built a successful business from the ground up have made a personal impact on the business— every day. Personal interaction is the most ancient form of communication, and it is still the most powerful." Jeff Galloway, US Olympian, Founder of Galloway Run/Walk Training Method, and Owner of Phidippides Running Store, Atlanta, GA

Everyone is unique. Everyone has qualities that set them apart from others. If you own a business, serve as the marketing or PR director of a corporation, or are an individual who wants to stand out, think about your brand.

Your Brand

There are thousands of public relations firms[4] and corporations that offer similar services. There are thousands of individuals who are looking for a job.[5] What sets you apart?

I am an adjunct professor at Hofstra University. In my Digital Communications class, I ask the students to tell me what they are passionate about. This will help them develop their brand.

Here are some examples:

- Sports Stadiums
- Superheroes
- Airplanes
- Field Hockey
- Country Music

Students are usually passionate about entertainment, books and theatre. What I say is, "If you enjoy something and can focus on it all the time, then that is your brand."

I tell them just what I'm telling you — write a list of things you love, things you enjoy, and then list in order of priority.

Everyone could have a unique brand. Your CEO may be an expert in golf or may be a master chef. Whatever his/her passion, that's a way to set him/her apart from others in the same field.

Let's take a real example. I recently met with an attorney who is a 9X Ironman finisher and he has run 70+ marathons. Doesn't it make sense for him to use this to his advantage in business? I suggested to him that we may use this to help him establish himself as a lawyer who can always "tackle any problem."

Today, everyone needs a differentiator. By building a brand that is unique to you, it will set you apart from your competition.

Once you have found something that you love and that you are passionate about, or, makes you different from others in your profession, think about your audience. Take these questions into consideration when defining your brand:

- To whom do you want to market?
- Who will be attracted to your brand?
- Who will either buy from you or will want to employ you?
- What makes it special?
- Why is it relevant?
- Where would people see your brand?

Buyer Persona

Having a buyer persona enables you to pinpoint your target market. According to Hubspot,[6] a buyer persona is "a semi-fictional representation of your ideal customer based on market research and real data about your existing customers."

The buyer persona is an area that needs special attention.

- To whom will you be marketing?
- What do they look like?
- What is their name?
- What are their demographics? Are they college educated? Are they high net worth individuals? Tell me who they are.

Please take the time and think about this. Put the book down for a moment and think.

Okay, now tell me who that person is...

Is this person a he, a she or other?

How old is the person?

What does the person look like?

What is the person's ethnicity?

What are their business goals?

What do they do in their free time?

Where do they spend disposable money?

For me, I use Betty and Bob as my two target markets for my business. Bob is the CEO of a small corporation that has revenue of $1 to $10 million. He may be slightly overweight because he's working all the time, or he may be very fit because he is a type-A personality. He may like running and triathlons as I do, or he is the more adventurous type that likes to ride his bike cross country, or he goes mountain climbing. Betty is a little less physically active. She works all the time and is committed to her job. She is diligent and wants to see her company succeed. Her title is the marketing director or VP of marketing. She is similar to me in terms of education and work experience. I see her as middle-aged, between 35 and 60.

Take a moment. I want you create a similar sketch. Figure out who it is that you are targeting for your business, your product or service, or for a new job.

Now write it down. The best way to remember who you are targeting is to write it down.

Refer back to this from time to time and update it if necessary. By writing it down, it will help keep you in check so that you can strategically revise your digital branding message to incorporate any changes.

☝ My Observation...

Take time out to see how you can be different than your competitors. What sets you apart? Use your passion to differentiate yourself from the pack. Then, spend time figuring out the right buyer persona for your brand. Make sure to include this in your integrated marketing plan.

Once you do that, the tactics will fall into place. Read on to find out what tactics should be incorporated into your integrated marketing plan.

PUTTING THE PIECES TOGETHER – BUILDING AN INTEGRATED MARKETING PLAN

"In today's digital world, putting all the pieces together in a well-organized plan will help you fully develop your brand and enable you to implement it in a systematic way." Hilary JM Topper, MPA, Author, ***"Everything you Ever Wanted to Know About Social Media, but were afraid to ask...Building Your Business Using Consumer Generated Media"*** Long Beach, NY

An integrated marketing plan is a roadmap that keeps you on target. Without it, you will get sidetracked and won't be able to accomplish your goals. Specifically, it is a campaign that takes your brand and uses it throughout everything you do in your business. The end result should be when you see your logo or your tag line, your consumers should think about your business. For example, you see the Nike swoosh, you know it is a Nike brand because you've seen the swoosh in advertisements, online and in retail shops. If you think this was by accident, think again. Nike's brand marketing team probably spent many months, maybe even years, developing this brand image to reflect who they are.

Your integrated marketing plan could be a one-year or a five-year program that will help you get your message to the community and build your brand.

According to "The Balance, Small Business Blog,"[7] "integrated marketing takes a holistic approach to making sure your brand is consistent." When something is consistent and your community sees it often, they end up recognizing your brand.

As a personal example, at HJMT Public Relations, we use the slogan, "We Love Attention." This slogan appears on everything that we do along with our bold logo, which has four different colors for each letter. Our hope is that when prospective clients see our logo, they think this is the attention-getting PR firm.

In the integrated marketing campaign that you are developing for your brand, include:

- **Goals** – What do you want to accomplish? How much do you want to sell this year? How much visibility do you want?
- **Objective** – How will you reach your goals?
- **Strategies** – How will you go about reaching your goals? Give an overall example here.
- **Target audience** – Who is it that you are targeting?
- **Tactics** – Which tactics will you incorporate to reach your goals? Tactics can include but are not limited to:

o **Social Media Marketing** – Which sites will you use to reach your target audience? How often will you post? What time will you post? How will you grow your community? How will you engage your community?

o **Blogging** – Should you blog? Should you guest blog? Should you create an ambassador program to help you spread the word about your brand?

o **Podcasting** – Does it make sense to create a video podcast? How about an audio podcast? Who will your guests be? What will the topics include?

o **Public Relations** – Should traditional PR be incorporated into the plan? Which publications should you target? What types of pitch letters or press releases will you produce? How will you follow up?

o **Graphic Identity** – Should you include a logo? Should you use the logo throughout your materials?

o **Digital Advertising** – Should you advertise on the web? What will it do for you?

o **Direct Mail and Email Marketing** – Should you incorporate these tools into your plan? Do you have mailing lists? Do you have material that you want to share?

o **Data Visualization and Photography** – What images will you use to help get your message out?

o **Contests and Promotions** – Should you have a contest or promotion? Will that help you reach your goal?

o **Experiential Marketing** – Should you create an event that will help you achieve your goals? Would it be beneficial to you to have your target audience meet you in person?

o   **Wearable Technology or The Internet of Things (IoT)** – How will you incorporate these elements into your marketing program? Should you include? What if you don't incorporate?

o   **Return on Investment**– Will you get a decent return? What are you anticipating?

Take some time and figure out what your integrated marketing plan is, so that you can start to implement. Make sure to go back and fine tune your plan every month.

👍 **My Observation…**

Finding the time to develop an integrated marketing plan is going to be a challenge, no matter if you just launched a start-up company or you operate a well-established business. Writing this book was a challenge for me. But, I was determined that if I could spend at least one hour a day, I could write it. Set aside the time, and you will see progress. Good luck to you!

TECHNOLOGY KILLED
THE PRESS RELEASE

"We have changed the traditional "press release" to "content" – there's still information to get out that our audiences need, and the format is an excellent and transparent way to inform. The press release isn't as vital and singular a tool as it once was, back when "publicity" and "media relations" were synonymous with "public relations." The release is just one tool in the box; and the media only one of our audiences." Melissa Connolly, Vice President, University Relations, Hofstra University, Hempstead, NY

To understand why technology killed the press release, we must take a look back. Public relations has been around since the beginning of time when the caveman wrote on cave walls to communicate ideas to others.

In 1906 when Ivy Lee[8] wrote the first press release as a result of a major train accident that occurred in Atlantic City, public relations was born. Ivy Lee was credited with alleviating the crisis, and he sent out the first known press release to the media.

It wasn't until Edward Bernays worked up a campaign for a cigarette company. Bernays hired women to march while smoking cigarettes. This was called, "torches of freedom"[9] campaign and took place during the Easter Sunday Parade of 1929. It was a significant moment for fighting social barriers for women smokers. The campaign created so much buzz it helped make cigarettes more acceptable for women and put Bernays in a positive light to generate more publicity for other major brands.

☝ What is a Press Release?

A press release is a statement issued to the media. It provides the "Who, What, Where, Why, When and How" in the first paragraph. Following that, is a quote or some background information. It is written like an inverted pyramid, with the essential information first followed by the least important information.

It is considered a news story or news item that is written by public relations professionals and sent to the media to entice them to write or broadcast a story about a particular topic.

The press release was never intended to be used in a newspaper or magazine verbatim. The goal of a press release has been and always will be to entice a reporter or producer to write a story.

☼ How Has It Changed?

Years ago, when I started in the field, a press release was typically three to five pages. Today, it's barely a page. Reporters and producers, just like consumers, have limited time to read. So, it's crucial to capture the essence of the story quickly and efficiently.

Today, many reporters don't even want a press release. They would prefer a "pitch" or a tweet in 280 characters or less.

The other thing that has changed with the introduction of social media is that public relations professionals are now dealing directly with the consumers. Social media gives the PR field, which hasn't changed much since the early 1900s, a new twist.

☼ What Are Newsrooms and Do We Need Them?

Many large and small businesses are creating newsrooms on their websites for their press materials. Then, they share it on social media sites, which link back to the website or blogsite on which it is posted.

PR practitioners continue to use newsrooms, but now we also send a tweet or a short, succinct email pitch to a producer or reporter. If the producer or reporter is interested, they will ask you for additional information, which you can provide by sending them back to your newsroom.

Clients and organizations today still feel they want a press release. A press release is not necessary and should only be used if there is a breaking news story. Otherwise, a tweet or short email pitch is perfect.

☝ My Observation...

Clients love press releases, so public relations practitioners need to know how to write them. However, media seldom use press releases in their stories unless the release is from a governmental agency, district attorney's office, or hospital, and it is breaking news. Therefore, a good pitch or a tweet may be more relevant than an actual press release to get media attention for your brand.

Publicity is one of the key tactics that should be included in an integrated marketing plan. Whether you are promoting a product to appear in a major women's magazine, or becoming a thought-leader in a trade publication by providing a bylined article, Public Relations is key to building your brand. I would highly suggest adding PR to your integrated marketing plan.

CONS

CONSUMERS ARE NOW
THE MEDIA...

*"As a member of X's and Instagram's first name club, I've seen
how much it's evolved as the media landscape has changed. Since
68% of Americans now get their news on social media (according
to a study by Pew Research Center), businesses have had to adapt
and focus on their social presence, now more than ever before.
A brand can travel in a single tweet and connect with millions
of their consumers. Take the #NuggsforCarter incident on X
[where a teen sought to get 18 million re-Tweets and free chicken
nuggets for a year] ... Because that hashtag generated billions
of impressions, it spawned a wave of global media coverage,
interviews, congratulatory Tweets, and social conversation for
Wendy's. Fifteen years ago, this would've been unimaginable."*
Gregory Galant, CEO and Co-Founder, MuckRack, NYC

Look around. It seems as if everyone has a mobile device.
No matter how rich, how poor, how young or how old, most
people have a mobile device. Statista suggests that there will
be more than 3.8 billion smart phones sold in 2021.[10] This

device is so powerful that 2.5 quintillion bytes of data are created daily. That's a lot of streaming.

If you go out on the street, if you go anywhere for that matter, you are probably being filmed by someone. Move over Google Glass; someone is filming you and you not aware. You will appear in an Instagram photo, a Snapchat video, live stream Facebook video or maybe even a security camera and there's nothing you can do about it.

Consumers are citizen journalists. They are looking, watching, and waiting for something to happen so that they can capture it.

I find myself doing that too. I pull out my iPhone, and I record an Instagram story or, I start live streaming on Facebook Live. I take mental notes and blog about it later.

Why? I am a citizen journalist and so are you.

During the season, I went to a New York Mets game with my family. I saw an entertainer playing his saxophone as we entered the stadium. I recorded him. He turned around and ran after me and recorded me. I think he wanted to show me how it felt, but interestingly, I didn't care.

That is why, when you talk about privacy, there is none any longer. When you post on social media about going on vacation, everyone knows. When you post about going on a date or buying a new dog, the whole world knows about it. To me, it seems like everyone is posting on Facebook or other social networking sites about everything that is happening in their lives.

At a local running event, a woman approached me and hugged me. "Hilary, it's so good to see you," she said. "I follow you on social, see everything you are doing and feel very close to you."

So how can you keep your life private? The only way is for you and your friends to never post and to have no digital footprint. However, that won't happen. There will always be someone in your community who will tag you or talk about you.

What do you do? You embrace it and let it happen.

Instead of getting caught up, think of ways to create videos, infographics and photographs that will reflect you and your brand in a positive light. Go back to the chapter on "Who Are You – Your Personal Brand" and think about your buyer persona and how you want to be portrayed in social media. Take that brand and run with it. Post what interests you.

☝ How IoT Relates To Business...

Many business owners may not see the value of the Internet of Things (IoT) and wearable technology, but if they don't acknowledge it, they will be lost in the shuffle.

IoT is a phrase that means that everything is connected. For instance, in my house, I have an Amazon Echo. When I know we are low on eggs at home, I say, "Alexa, add eggs to the shopping list."

Alexa is also connected to my Philips Hue lights. When I watched a connected show like "12 Monkeys," my lights automatically change depending on the scene. This enabled my family and me to get more into the show. I also have a Nest that links with my iPhone so that I can turn up or down the air conditioning or the heat, from anywhere at any time. Most recently, we purchased a few Sonos speakers for our home, and now we have surround sound, operated through either Alexa or the iPhone app.

Even my television is connected to Alexa. When I asked Alexa, "who is Hilary Topper?" she responded with:

"Hilary JM Topper is an American podcaster, media consultant, blogger, publicist, author, entrepreneur, and triathlete."

It's just crazy how we are so connected that our devices are starting to know who we are! This opens doors for brands like yours and mine. By having a simple Wikipedia page, Alexa could know who you are too.

You can even drive up to your house and through your mobile device or your wearable technology, you can pre-heat the oven or start the laundry. Companies like Lowes, Nest, Google, and others are constantly developing these types of products, and we're going to become more connected as time goes by.

What about the guy who crossed the English Channel on a hoverboard?[11] Can you see where this is going?

Technology is rapidly changing the way we communicate and do business, and by keeping up with the significant online sources, you will be ahead of the crowd.

Take a look at how popular the fitness trackers are. There are so many companies that make fitness trackers, and for the most part, they all do the same thing. People are religious about wearing them daily. Then, they share with their social community. This connects to branding because these folks are your consumers who are sharing and in turn are buying your product.

I use the Garmin Epix. This watch connects with Strava, a popular running and triathlon social site that tracks your workouts, and people give "kudos" to each other. The watch also connects to Garmin Connect, Training Peaks and Final Surge, programs that enable my coach to see my workout during and after I've completed it. There is a tracking device that allows them to watch as I do it. As a running coach, I also see all of my athletes' activities on Final Surge in real time.

Strava enables you to see how others are performing, and offers the encouragement of others, which helps motivate you.

Today, new wearable products are coming out daily.[12] There is a pet tracker so that if your dog gets lost, you can find him. There is a wearable tattoo to track your vital signs. There is even wearable clothing that lights up and can display words or phrases through the use of an app.

With wearables and IoT, the possibilities are endless. You now can reach your consumer in so many different ways, through apps, through IoT, and through wearables. This technology keeps evolving, and you will need to continue to grow with it.

♥ An Original Google Glass Explorer Talks About Glass

I am an original Google Glass explorer. At the time, it was a big deal. Now, not so much.

Google made a dynamic wearable product that enabled me, and thousands of others who were in the program, to access the internet and share photos and video with our social communities as experiences were happening. We were also able to access various apps that allowed us to interpret signage in multiple languages because the technology converted them into our native tongue. If we wore Google Glass during a run or bike ride, we were able to track our workout performance in real time by seeing the stats in the viewfinder above our eyes. In addition to that, we could ask "Glass" to find various places to eat or get the news instantaneously.

Many would say that Glass did the same thing as a smartphone. I'll admit that is true. However, having Glass on your face gave you a convenience that is inaccessible with a smartphone.

As for the backlash, I'm still not quite sure there was any. Anywhere that I went, I never felt unaccepted. On the contrary, people would stop me on the street and ask me what I had on my face. Some people even asked if they could try it on. I found it exceptionally interesting when I went to Napa Valley, California, and most of the people I met had never seen a pair of Google Glass, even with Silicon Valley being so close.

No one asked me to take off my Google Glass. When I went to concerts, I was wearing it, and my friends were holding up their mobile phones to take photos and record the concert.

They were asked to put away their phones. No one ever stopped me from taking pictures or video with Glass.

Google Glass wasn't accessible to the masses. The only way to get it was to either be a journalist, celebrity or be really wealthy. In the hopes that I could get my hands on it, I entered a X contest they were hosting in early 2013 called, "#IfIHadGlass." Followers were asked to tweet what they would do if they had Google Glass. In my first submission, I wrote:

"#IfIHadGlass I would wear them during the Diva Half Marathon and film along the way."

I didn't hear from Google until I tweeted, "I want my Google Glass more than my MTV!"

From July 2013 when I picked up my first pair of Glass until now, I thought that my second submission was how I got into the program, but after seeing Glass Vol 001, which was a digital booklet to honor the Google Glass explorer program, I realized my first submission is how I qualified. You see, they used my quote in the booklet. That was exciting.

When I first picked up Google Glass in Chelsea, I felt as if I had walked into the Starship Enterprise. Everyone wore Glass. It was one of the most exciting experiences I have ever had. I was shown how to use Glass, and my next challenge was what to do with it.

At first, I wasn't quite sure. I wanted to incorporate Glass into my PR firm and use it to help clients get attention.

I was part of a Google Glass exploration and flew down to The Beaches of Ft. Myers and Sanibel,[13] along with four other explorers. We were challenged to film and photograph the area and the person who did the most using the hashtag "#FindYourIsland" and "FtMyerSanibel" were given a free trip to go back. Unfortunately, I didn't win the trip, but I helped the tourism board get more than 70 million impressions on social media within the first week of us being there.

In addition to that, my staff and I decided to film a reality show using Google Glass and a handheld camera. The show, "Glasslandia,"[14] had six episodes and focused on HJMT PR and one client. The show was a huge hit and had more than 60 million impressions on the internet.

Each week, we debuted an episode followed by a live X chat with the HJMT staff that was a part of the series. One staff member was promoted, and another was hired. I filmed boxing at a local gym and running on the Long Beach boardwalk wearing Glass. I still have people asking me about the show and when I will shoot Season 2. And at a recent CES convention in Las Vegas, another Google Glass explorer told me that Google watched every episode with popcorn in hand. That was pretty thrilling for me to hear!

I later took Glass to another level by realizing that the technology, maybe not in its current form, would be the wave of the future. It introduced me to the whole wearable market and enabled me to host and produce two additional web shows, "Wearable on Air" and "Tech News Now." And perhaps most importantly, it helped me build relationships with forward-thinkers who shared my interest in technology.

"Wearable on Air" was a live Google Hangout where I interviewed CEOs of wearable companies. I have had representatives from Pebble (one of the original smart watches) and Vuzix (a company that makes wearable headsets) among others on the show.

"Tech News Now," which merged with my NY lifestyle blog, "HilaryTopper.com,"[15] has enabled me to review tech products and film and interview various people on wearable tech and the Internet of Things.

I'm a little sad the program is over, but I'm excited about the future of wearables and can't wait to see what's in store next.

↻ My Observation...

Consumers are now the media. Everyone has a mobile device and look at their device several times a day, not only to see what their friends are doing but also to see what is happening in the world around them. When there's a breaking news story, most people know about it immediately through their mobile devices. With technology changing at rapid speeds, it's imperative to stay on top of how people get their information and communicate with each other in order to continuously build your brand. And, as we continuously connect with our home appliances, our fitness trackers and such, we must adapt and build our brand to incorporate those products as well. If it's not advertising on Alexa, it may be partnering with a technology brand to get your message in the ear of the consumer. As we are more and more on our mobile devices, it may make sense to target PR or advertising opportunities on these devices.

MED

MEDIA'S ROLE IN DIGITAL BRANDING?

"Now, credible news appears side-by-side with misinformation, disinformation, and actual fake news. The onus is on the news consumer to have the skills to figure it all out. Knowing how to navigate today's media landscape successfully enables you to become a world-class citizen." Jaci Clement, CEO and Executive Director, Fair Media Council, Long Island, NY

From the time Paul Revere made his midnight ride, the media has always played an essential role in the lives of Americans.

Consider the scholar Marshall McLuhan, who said, "The medium is the message."[16] For the longest time, the medium had controlled the message. It had the power to persuade us to eat particular foods, wear certain clothes, and vacation at specific destinations. If the media told consumers to buy a product or service, the stores could not keep up with the demands. Endorsements were aplenty.

However, rapid improvements in technology have changed the way we get our news. Technology also changes the way we digest our news. For example, how many people do you know under the age of 30 who read a traditional print newspaper? More and more people are turning to their personal computers, tablets, and mobile devices to get information. Every day, newspapers and magazines close their print versions. Online media, on the other hand, has become more prevalent.

Power has shifted from the media into the hands of the consumer.[17] Through the widespread use of the internet, social media sites and blogs, key consumers are spreading their message and making the decisions that are affecting all of our lives. There are consumers' blogs about every subject and product imaginable, and readers look to these bloggers as the experts in their fields.

Publicists and corporations used to shower reporters and producers with gifts so that the media would try out their products. Today, bloggers get bombarded with such gifts. New restaurant owners want bloggers to come to their restaurants to enjoy a meal out and then blog about it. Savvy restaurateurs know that if dozens of bloggers write about their dining spots, people will eat there. In the movie, "Field of Dreams," Kevin Costner is told, "if you build it, he will come." So rings true the power of the influencer.

Articles are now appearing in traditional media for bloggers interested in testing various products. For example, *Laptop Magazine*[18] featured an article in which a coffee company was looking for bloggers to test their coffee. When I contacted the manufacturer, they sent me multiple types of coffee to test out, which I did and then blogged about it.

People now communicate through social networking. Politics has become indicative of this. Remember the 2008 presidential campaign? President Barack Obama is still called President 2.0 because of his savvy social media plan. He had blogs, podcasts, video podcasts, social networking sites, and more to get young people to vote for him in this historic election. Supporters helped him spread his message via viral marketing.

Now, President Donald Trump uses X as his messenger. If he is angry about something, he Tweets about it. If the president has a position on policy, he Tweets about that too. He sends out Tweets daily, which helped X resurrect its brand. Is it a good thing or a bad thing? You decide.

☝ The Future of News Media

Although the consumer blog is essential, traditional media still plays a significant role in society. Some worry that there will be no offline versions of major newspapers, but I think otherwise because news media is still a source of reputable information. However, there will be fewer and fewer community newspapers, and the major newspapers will become very thin, due to a lack of advertising revenues.

Also, what about television? With the addition of digital video recorders, a vastly increasing number of people are fast-forwarding through commercials to get the information they want. This, in turn, diminishes advertising revenue. Big corporations are learning that television advertising is not productive anymore. Today, most television shows can now be seen in full online, on the station's website or through Hulu. Although there are some ads online, you can often fast forward through those too.

Most Millennials and Gen Z'ers watch YouTube. According to a recent Pew Research study,[19] 85% of all teens use YouTube. They learn new things there, they watch gaming shows, and they take a break from being a teen.

Corporations, non-profit organizations, and small businesses need to be more niche-centric. Advertising on blogs, forums, wikis, and news media sites may prove to be the more effective and efficient way to go. By doing so, advertisers can accurately pinpoint their audience and get a better return on investment.

☝ The Future of Public Relations

Public relations prompts people to speak with others about issues and topics. For example, someone posts a microblog, and people throughout the community respond. Public relations gets people to talk to each other to create word-of-mouth publicity, which helps build communities. The more you post and have comments, the more you will see your community grow.

Public relations is changing, as people find new communities that bring them together. Take a look at Alltop.com, a site created by Guy Kawasaki. Here, you can find links to articles indexed properly and written by various authors on particular topics ranging from lifestyle and business to people and sports. This resource puts editors, reporters, and bloggers at your fingertips whether you are a PR professional or a business owner doing publicity on your own.

You will also see an increasing number of PR firms creating their newsrooms. Here, as discussed earlier in the book, journalists can search for relevant stories and get story ideas. Instead of spamming reporters, editors, and producers, we now send out short teasers via social networking sites and emails to all the targeted reporters. If they are interested, they can look on the site and get all the information they need. The site becomes more of a resource for them. They also have an opportunity to ask questions or look for other sources.

☙ **My Observation...**

Since more people are turning to the web for their information, business owners need to rethink their ways of getting their message out. Consider posting releases on an online newsroom, targeting bloggers, running contests on YouTube, or setting up groups on Facebook or LinkedIn. You may even consider hiring an influencer to help promote your message. The strategies of the past are no longer enough. We now need to adapt, adjust, and think of new tactics to reach your market via the internet.

A FEW WORDS ABOUT DEVELOPING A GRAPHIC IDENTITY CAMPAIGN

"A graphic identity campaign is very important. It communicates a look, a personality and a vibe for your business. It's the first impression everyone gets, and instantly gives a customer a sense of confidence and trust in you or your business." Jonathan E. Gicewicz, Owner, JEG Design Inc., Burlington, VT

Have you ever noticed that there are some companies, usually smaller companies, that have no graphic identity and everything they do is disheveled?

When you have a business or a brand, it's important to keep everything consistent including your graphics. Here are important tactics to incorporate:

- Choose a color palette.
- Use color psychology to pick a shade that matches your graphic identity as identified in the quote above.

- Choose your typography with no more than two complementary fonts that represent your brand in order to keep it attractive and simple.
- Define imagery choices that appeal to you and those that don't.
- Create a branding guide, a booklet that outlines your logo, color choices, photography, imagery and create a graphic standard for your brand.

Having a branding guide is key. In it, include all of the above and also make sure the positioning of the logo is included.

When I worked for non-profit organizations, in addition to showing how the logo should appear in advertisements, social media pages, business cards, and letterhead, we also included how the logo should look on signage such as trucks, billboards and benches. Placement was also a big issue. The placement had to be consistent in everything we did. This enabled us to keep the brand's logo on point.

When you look at colors for your brand remember each color represents something to your consumers.

- Green = Organic, Prosperous
- Blue = Trust, Strength, Dependable
- Purple = Creativity, Luxurious, Wise
- Red = Vitality, Bold, Active, Youthful
- Orange = Confidence, Happy, Friendly
- Yellow = Optimism, Clear, Energetic
- Gray = Balance, Prestigious, Peaceful, Calm

If you don't have a designer and want to prepare a graphic identity campaign for your brand, use tools like Adobe Illustrator or choose a free program like Canva to help you design a logo.

Many people use online sites like 99Designs to help develop a logo and branding campaign. It's very inexpensive and can be a good option for some who are first starting out. When I developed a brand for my triathlon team, WeRTriathletes,[20] and for my Galloway running club, Team Galloway Long Island,[21] I hired 99Designs to create a logo for me. Artists submitted several dozen designs before I chose the ones I loved and currently use for those brands.

For WeRTriathletes, I wanted to have a strong, graffiti look. When people saw the brand, I wanted them to feel empowered. On the other hand, when I developed the Team Galloway Long Island logo with 99Designs, I asked them for an inviting, inclusive logo that was also fun.

✆ **My Observation...**

When you embark on a graphic identity campaign, make sure that everything is consistent. The logo should appear everywhere, including your letterhead, business cards, proposals, signage, social media sites, blogs, everywhere. This will help you brand your materials. When you see the logo for Starbucks, it doesn't have the words Starbucks in the logo. But, when you see it, you think coffee. That's what you want to achieve with your brand.

Make sure that these graphics appear on everything you do, including online sources, press materials, brochures, direct mail and email marketing. Graphic identity should be including in your integrated marketing plan in the tactics section.

SEARCH ENGINE OPTIMIZATION

"Having SEO [Search Engine Optimization] helps with directing and garnering further organic traffic and getting more qualified eyes on your site. SEO is not just about search engines but improving user experience and usability of the site overall. Most trust from search engine users is found within an established presence in top positions for relevant search queries. SEO can be measured through analytics reporting such as Google Analytics that provides a vast myriad of avenues to track user flow and content performance. The success of an online business or site will rely heavily on its ranking in SEO and ability to map, view, and use data within Google Analytics." Ken Braun, President, Lounge Lizard, NYC, Long Island, NY, and Los Angeles, CA

Today, everything is about being first on the search engines. Search Engine Optimization or SEO affects the visibility of a website on the search engines. This process is also called natural, organic, or earned, and it can make or break your business.

If someone is searching for a plumber in your area and types into Google, "Plumber near me," that person will get a list of local plumbers. However, if a business isn't on the first page and falls on the second or third pages of a search, the company is not likely to be found.

How Does SEO Work?

Although the algorithms continuously change, there are currently two ways to get higher rankings on the search engines. Google looks at your website's content and the way it was built. It also looks at how many linkbacks you have from other credible sites. Search engines, no matter which one you use, consist of crawlers (also known as spiders or bots), the index, which stores data for the search engines, and the algorithm. Unfortunately for marketers and SEO folks, the algorithm is kept secret by Google. Once someone can break into the code, Google changes it to be fair to all brands/businesses.

Google looks at the frequency and location of your keywords on your website. If a keyword only appears once throughout the site, it will receive a lower score from Google. Keywords should be placed throughout your site, on your images, on your home page copy and more.

The search engine also looks at how long the website has existed. Google puts a value on the length of time the site has been live. So, a new site will receive a lower score than a site that has been around for 10 years.

Finally, link building (or what some people call backlinks) is important. The more web pages linked to your site, the better. That is why free directories and putting ads on blog sites are essential. If there is a link from one website to another, it is useful and helps with natural or organic SEO. It's essential that your site links to another high-quality site; otherwise, the links won't be worth anything.

According to *Search Engine Watch,*[22] an online SEO publication, relevant links can be created through these tactics:

- Use HARO (see definition in glossary at the end of the book) – to find stories that you can be a resource for in hopes that once it's published you will get an authoritative backlink.
- Prepare guest blogs with backlinks.
- Co-author an online article or blog.
- Link to other valuable sites including blogs with ads or "paid for" links.
- Put a blog on your website.
- Use link-building directories.

♂ Keywords – How To Choose Them?

Think about your business. What would someone type into Google if they wanted your service? For me, it might be "public relations Long Island." So, "public relations Long Island" would be a "long-tail keyword" that I would use in my site to help me with my SEO.

Make sure that you develop a list of at least 10 long-tail keywords. Long-tail keywords refer to a grouping of words, rather than one word, that someone might use in a search. And with the prevalence of Amazon Echo, Google Home, or even Apple's Siri, people tend to phrase a search inquiry in the form of a question. Going back to my industry, someone might key in "What is the best public relations firm on Long Island?" I haven't checked, but hopefully, it's HJMT.

A caution about keywords: never stuff them into your site. Otherwise, Google could potentially ban you. Use keywords often, but make sure that they work in your copy.

Other things to consider when developing keywords:

Which terms do your competitors use?

How does your content perform? Are people reading your blogs?

Make sure to use geo-locations.

☝ User Experience

Since 2018, Google has considered user experience as a way to move companies up the SEO ladder. Make sure that when you build your site, it's user-friendly and interactive. The goal here is to have users visit, stay, and then link to your site. The more people that stay on your website, the more likely Google's algorithms will deem it a good result, giving it a higher ranking.

According to *Forbes Magazine*,[23] "try to optimize your mobile search and browsing." More than 50% of all searches are done on a mobile device. More people are searching on mobile devices than ever before. Also, optimize for video and images, and make sure that you optimize for voice.

⚫ Other Tips to Consider

- Make sure to shorten your URLs. You can use a tool like Bit.ly and gain data by evaluating the clicks.
- If you are developing your long-tail keywords, include your geo-location. Customers search by location.
- Focus on your website's user experience. Is it an enjoyable experience? Is it easy to use? Encourage comments on your site to help you understand how people assess their user experience on your site.
- Use keywords within your site or as titles for your blogs.
- Optimize your website for speed.
- Use unique data.
- Get backlinks from podcasts.

⚫ How Do You Get Backlinks (or Linkbacks)?

There are lots of ways to get linkbacks. Some of the more popular methods include:

- **Free directories** — Search on Google for free directories.
- **Blogs** — Be sure to link to another blog entry on your site, known as an "internal link," and to another website, or an "external link."
- **Press releases** — The traditional press release isn't what it used to be. Today, it should have links to pages on your site to help your site with its SEO.
- **Online publications** — Consider writing a piece for an online magazine and then get a linkback to your

site. Linkbacks are just as good if not better than getting paid to write a blog post.

- **Hashtags** — Use hashtags in your social posts with the keywords from your site to help your site get better SEO.

☝ Google Knowledge Graph

Have you ever noticed that when you type a search term into Google, you see a list of relevant answers on the left side, and on the right side, you see a logo along with a description in which you are searching? This is called the Google Knowledge Graph,[24] and it's instrumental in SEO.

For example, when you type in "Star Trek," you will see on the left side, videos, and below the videos, the official Star Trek website. And on the right side, the Google Knowledge Graph. Having a Google Knowledge Graph will strengthen your brand.

Having your website appear on a Google Knowledge Graph may not always happen. However, below are some steps to increase your chances.

☝ Step 1:

Position keywords so that they appear in the title, URL, meta description, image/image description, in the introduction of your website, and throughout the content. But be careful. Don't overdo it with the keywords. Use them where they make sense.

☝ Step 2:

Write a catchy headline and sub-headline. Use bullets because they are easier to read. Have a call-to-action at the end.

☝ Step 3:

Incorporate a strong web design, with bold headlines. Also, make sure to use pertinent data, including graphs and charts. On social, be active and link back to your website from your social posts.

☝ Step 4:

Consider using Schema.org as a plugin to your website. This plugin will help with essential coding to increase your search engine optimization. Don't forget to incorporate some quality linkbacks. If you don't have a wiki page, create one. This will improve your chances of getting a Google Knowledge Graph. Finally, register for online databases and make sure your social sites are current and active.

☝ Google Analytics

When clients tell me, they don't look at Google Analytics, I shake my head. Why isn't anyone looking at one of the most vital tools that we have on the web that is FREE???

Google Analytics is a powerful tool that helps you evaluate who is coming to your site, how often, what they are looking at, where they are from, and more. By knowing this information about your consumers, you can tailor your site to fit their needs.

For example, I noticed on my ATriathletesDiary.com[25] blog that I have hundreds of people looking at my swim chart every day. Knowing this information leads me to believe that people want to read about anything swimming related. So, I tailored some additional blog entries to address that and have been seeing a good return on my investment by getting more subscribers.

With a couple of clicks, you will see:

- How many people are looking at your site.
- The ages of the people visiting.
- The demographics including their geographic locations, with the ability to delve further by pinpointing nation, region, county and so on; interests, and sometimes even their sexual orientation.
- Where they are coming from, via linkbacks from referral sites.
- Whether your social media efforts are working and if they are generating consumers.

There are other tools besides Google Analytics that offer similar features, including software such as Awstats and Webalizer. These tools are placed on your site through your host company. They may have more significant numbers than Google Analytics because they take into account everyone coming to your site.

☝ G4

G4, also known as Google Analytics 4, represents a significant evolution in the world of digital branding and marketing analytics. Unlike its predecessor, Universal Analytics, G4 focuses on providing insights based on customer-centric measurement, rather than session-based data. This shift allows brands to understand their audience's journey across various devices and platforms in a more unified way, enabling them to create highly personalized brand experiences.[102]

In contrast, Universal Analytics primarily focuses on sessions or website visits. While it offers valuable insights into user behavior, it lacks the predictive capabilities and cross-platform tracking that G4 provides.

Branding in a digital world involves understanding and reaching your audience where they are and how they interact with your brand. G4's advanced features like AI-powered insights and more comprehensive data controls make it an invaluable tool for modern digital branding. It empowers brands to anticipate future actions their customers might take, offering a more proactive approach to brand engagement.[103]

☝ My Observation...

When you build a website, make sure to incorporate it with Google Analytics. You can refer to the host analytics as well, but Google will take you deeper into the demographics of the consumer reading your website. Use long-tail keywords and get the backlinks wherever and whenever possible. Invest your money into linkbacks, especially blogs and online directories. This is a vital tool for increasing your rank on the search engines.

Tip: The Americans with Disabilities Act (ADA) has been an advocate for ensuring that physical spaces are compliant for people with disabilities. Make sure that your website is compliant as well as your physical space.

Remember, include SEO in your integrated marketing plan.

CREATING AN EXCEPTIONAL EXPERIENCE FOR YOUR CUSTOMERS

"When creating a branded experience for any client, it is important to manifest their vision but set clear expectations on what the client presence and branding will look like. For consumer and media events, the brand should always be the focal point – but creating an authentic environment for outsiders is a key driver for success. At the start of developing event executional plans, ensure the look and feel of the event meets the client's vision but branding is not overtly hitting the attendee over the head. Soft and authentic branding touches are always preferred!" Thomas Pallidino, Public Relations and Social Media Professional, NYC

Years ago, my firm used to organize lots of events, and sometimes we still do. We would be assigned a task, such as arranging a golf outing or gala. Then, we would come back and brainstorm how to make these events more of an

experience so that clients' consumers would keep coming back.

Experiential marketing is a term that describes an experience that offers a unique way to connect with consumers.

Hubspot[26] offers the following definition: "experiential marketing, also called 'engagement marketing,' is a marketing strategy that invites an audience to interact with a business in a real-world situation. Using participatory, hands-on, and tangible branding material, the market can show its customers not just what the company offers, but what it stands for."

In 2016, we rented CitiField in Queens and held the NY TRI EXPO. We solicited vendors and had 70 vendors, 20+ seminars geared for all levels of triathletes, and lots of contests. This massive undertaking was completely branded from the website to every detail in the room. Everything had the logo or the colors of the logo so that the brand stayed on point. We even gave out goodie bags with the NY TRI EXPO logo, had temporary swim, bike, run tattoos and more. As a result, we had 2,000 people in attendance, 70 vendors and a whole lot of positive publicity that helped the firm get to its next level.

☍ How Do You Incorporate A Brand Into An Experiential Marketing Campaign?

Make sure to keep your brand on point. If the event warrants, create banners, tablecloths, even wear the brand's logo on your clothing. Students in my Hofstra PR Campaigns class, organized an event for their non-profit client. They made sure that the colors were consistent with the brand and that everything coordinated down to the drinks they served and the cake they had on the table. They even had swag that reflected the client's brand.

☌ Examples of Large Corporations Embracing Experiential Marketing

Coca-Cola

In celebration of the 2018 FIFA World Cup,[27] Coca-Cola Company conducted an augmented reality experience outside of the Zurich main train station. Consumers had the opportunity to "show off their skills" with Switzerland's top soccer player, Xherdan Shaqiri. They also were able to take a photo with him and enter a contest to be eligible to win the official match ball of the FIFA World Cup. This experience engaged soccer fans and gave them a memory tied to the Coca-Cola brand.

Refinery29

Refinery29 is a website specifically for women who want to know how to live a stylish, well-rounded life. The site includes entertainment news, fashion tips, health, and more. For the past few years, the site has hosted their 29Rooms[28] event, which is more like a funhouse for adults. These events, held in Washington, D.C., LA and NYC, feature 29 stand-alone rooms, each of them different. The experience was all hands-on, so a participant might walk into a room with a big typewriter and have the opportunity to type by jumping from one letter to the next. And another room might feature punching bags and offer consumers boxing gloves. By hosting an event such as this, more people were able to understand Refinery29 as a brand and in turn, visit their website on a regular basis.

Volkswagen

Another engaging experiential marketing campaign came from Volkswagen[29] when the automaker turned a typical staircase in a popular subway station in Stockholm, Sweden, into a giant piano. Volkswagen's goal was to offer a fun event that also inspired more people to take the stairs as opposed to the escalator to tie back to their sustainability efforts. During this campaign, 66% more people chose the stairs as a result, and Volkswagen garnered a reputation as an environmentally friendly vehicle.

☼ Experiential Marketing Tips

- Keep the experience memorable but on brand.
- Consider breaking a record to generate media interest and make participants feel invested in the experience.
- Think about hosting an event that offers suspense for consumers.
- Provide value so that consumers pay attention.
- Create branded hashtags that can be used in social media to generate more exposure.
- Consider partnering with another brand to expand your reach. This works best when both companies are complementary to each other.
- Ensure that the experience ties into your brand.
- Keep the experience focused, and remember that experiential marketing can work for both B2C and B2B.
- Consider hosting an experience at a conference or convention geared toward your target market.

☝ My Observation…

Experiential marketing can be a great asset in an integrated marketing plan. Be sure the event is branded and targets the right consumers. You can be as creative as you like here. The more creative you are, the more attention you will bring to your brand. Remember to promote via social, blogs, and podcasts to ensure ample awareness.

If you feel experiential marketing can benefit your brand, don't forget to put in your integrated marketing plan.

ARE YOU SOCIAL?

"My favorite networking site continues to be Instagram. I am a believer that the art of storytelling begins with visuals, and Instagram continues to build its platform to engage consumers across many categories that grabs their passion." Yanique Woodall, Head of Brand Communications, The Home Depot, Atlanta, GA

Social networking sites are places on the internet where people can interact directly with each other.

☝ According to Wikipedia:[30]

"Social networking sites focus on building online communities of people who share common interests and/or activities or who are interested in exploring the interests and actions of others. Most social networking sites are web-based and provide a variety of ways for users to interact, such as e-mail and instant messaging services. Social networking has created new ways to communicate and share information. Social networking websites are being used regularly by millions of people, and it now seems that social networking will be an enduring part of everyday life. Many social networking services contain directories of diverse categories (such as former classmates). These are meant to connect with friends (usually with self-description pages) and recommender systems linked to trust."

Once you start social networking, there will be sites you favor and frequent often. When I wrote my first book, I was using Plaxo, Facebook, LinkedIn, FriendFeed, X, Yammer, Flickr, and Seesmic. Today, I am mostly on Facebook, X, LinkedIn, and Instagram.

You need to determine which sites are right for you and right for your business. This is the first step in determining your social media plan and implementation strategy, all part of the integrated marketing plan.

There are hundreds of social networking sites on the internet. Most people know about the popular ones such as Facebook, X, and LinkedIn, but there are so many more out there. Each country has dozens of additional social networking sites as well. There are also social networking sites for individualized interests.

☝ Why Use Social Networking Sites?

Social networking sites enable people to get to know each other better. There are only so many hours in a day. Everyone has hectic lives. Social networking helps people connect more effectively and on a more personal level than any other forum.

For example, I have friends on Facebook that I could never initially connect with outside of an online community. This is a common occurrence among Facebook users. It's also a great tool to reconnect with people who you haven't seen in years. I have two childhood friends with whom I recently reconnected with on Facebook, and we have crossed over from the virtual world to the real world by meeting in person.

Still, sometimes people in the virtual world want to stay there. They don't want to cross over, and I find that fascinating. They want to talk with you on Facebook, but when you suggest getting together for coffee, they don't want to do it. Everyone has their reasons for being on these social networking sites. My goal is to strengthen my connections and build business for my public relations firm, so I enjoy meeting face-to-face. But, others find exclusively chatting online is satisfying.

Through social networking sites, I have gotten to know numerous people that I would otherwise not have had the chance to meet. I have also launched networking groups online and have met a lot of people that way. In 2009, I founded the Social Media Association. At that time, it enabled me to learn more about the people I met on social networking sites. I could see what we had in common, and gain insights about their interests, hobbies, or family. Then we met as a group each month to talk about new trends and our shared interests and develop a connection. Since I founded the group, it has gone through at least three sets of presidents and continues to thrive.

If you have a local social media group in your area, consider joining it. If there are no local groups to join, there are other ways to stay informed about the topic. There are multiple publications such as *Social Media Examiner* and *Mashable* that help keep you informed on all the new social networking sites and trends going on.

One key to using social networking sites to develop business is to create a community with others online. Evaluate the social networking websites and figure out which ones work for you. Perhaps four or five of them will seem beneficial, and the rest are irrelevant to your niche market. Or, you may want to be on as many social networking sites as possible. The key is to share contacts and create a community that will enable you to interact, get feedback, and learn what your consumers like and dislike.

Remember, each social networking site targets a different audience; however, most sites do share a lot of common ground, with most being more similar than they are different.

In subsequent chapters, we will explore various social networking sites. Read the information and then decide for yourself which sites make sense for your business. Then, remember to include these social networking sites in your integrated marketing plan. Lastly, in the plan, write down how often you will post, what content you will provide, and your call-to-action.

My Observation...

It's funny how Facebook, which was originally a site for college students, became the norm. If you're not on Facebook at this point, you have missed out on a lot. But, you have also kept yourself off the grid. If you have a brand that you want people to recognize then you need to have a social media plan incorporated into your integrated marketing plan.

USING SOCIAL MEDIA TO PROMOTE YOUR BUSINESS

"As a journalist, social media has become an indispensable tool for me. I use it to field both sources and stories. Now I have literally hundreds at my fingertips at any given time morning, noon or night. Bottom line is if you're not learning how to adapt with it, you'll definitely be at a disadvantage, especially in this digital world where social media is the new proverbial water cooler." Jamie Herzlich, New York Business Journalist and Columnist, Long Island, NY

Building a community takes time and patience. Start by joining a few critical social networking sites identified in the chapters that follow. Create a community within your sphere of influence, including your friends, your business associates, and your acquaintances. Build on that foundation by following your friends' friends. Soon, you will have dozens of people following you, and you will be following dozens of people. The more active you are on these online networking sites, the more people will want to be your friend on social media.

Make sure when you are building your community that you qualify the people that want to get involved. Here are some critical questions to ask when building a community:

- Why am I creating this community?
- What am I trying to promote?
- Who will use this site, and what will it do for them?
- Who will build this community? (One person should spearhead the effort.)
- Will members of my community interact with each other?
- What if my community criticizes my product or me? (You can't control your community because each member has a voice. The more a company welcomes—even celebrates criticism—the stronger it bonds to its community.)
- What ideas and opinions will you be sharing?
- How will you market and publicize the community?

By building a community and marketing your product or services to it, you will be known as an authority on the topic because you are the founder of the community. In other words, as the founder, you are the one with the knowledge on the subject, and it makes you the leader.

⟳ How Do You Get Started?

Start with one social networking site and work it. If you want, you can add a few more to make sure that you get a well-rounded audience. I know a woman who only uses LinkedIn, but she uses it to the fullest and builds her business using the one social networking site. You can do that too.

Before you start, speak with your clients and find out which social networking site(s) they use. Log onto your target sites and get started. Fill in all the pertinent information about yourself and your business. Make sure to put in all your business information, including your email address and mobile phone so that people can contact you. This information also adds credibility. You would be surprised to see how many people leave this vital information out.

In addition to joining social networking sites, you may consider setting up a blog. A blog could be about any subject area, from one of your areas of expertise to your lifestyle. On my blog, www.NYLifestyleBlog.com, I include information about life experience, restaurant reviews, product reviews, travel reviews, and more. I write this for a general audience. However, my ATriathletesDiary.com blog is especially for runners, cyclists, swimmers, and triathletes. It's more of a niche blog. I started this blog to share experiences with my community but I also wanted to connect on a personal level. The more people that connect with you personally, the more likely they are to want to do business with you. As a result of this blog, I have gained invaluable relationships and sponsorships.

When you only talk about one topic, it becomes limiting, and your readers will get bored. Find ways to keep things interesting by adding polls, utilizing guest bloggers and more. It also helps people get to know you and have a dialogue with you, which is the point of building a community. Besides, people like doing business with those they know and have similar interests.

On my social networking sites, I have a link to both of my blogs, my online radio show, Hilary Topper on Air,[31] My

YouTube Channel, and the HJMT[32] website (www.hjmt.com). Linking all of my sites together and then linking sites using keywords enables my blog to get more hits or readers.

When I started my blog in March 2008, I had 400 unique visitors after a month. In August 2011, my unique visitor counter hit nearly 30,000 unique visitors each month. Today, it has more than 88,000. My triathlon blog has 50,000 unique visitors, and my radio podcast has more than 230,000 listeners.

If you have multiple social networking sites, you can use Buffer, Sendible, Hootsuite, Hubspot, or a similar platform to maximize your efforts. These sites link all of your social networking sites together and enables you to post your updates once then filters that update to all the connected sites.

Market to your community and engage in conversations by using different features, including discussions, photos, videos, wall postings, reviews, and so on. Before you know it, you will be building an online community of followers and marketing to that community. This will entice your customers to learn more about you or the product offered. It makes a personal connection and engages your target audience and will lead to business.

✋ Social Media Plan

No matter what type of industry you are in, your organization should benefit from a social media plan. With your plan you should:

- Commit to at least one social networking site and work it!
- Enroll with an aggregator, or feed reader, like Sendible, Buffer, Hootsuite, or similar site, which is discussed above.
- Develop a blog that would attract your buyers.
- Guest blog on other sites that are relevant to your field or that target your particular market.
- Include podcasts and video podcasts in your plan.
- Maintain your social media activity. Get your message out as often as possible and be honest and credible, by adding supporting links to other sites that are reliable.

Once you implement the plan, it is critical to continue to be interactive with your community.

There is a fine line, though. If you post too much, you will be unfollowed. So, make sure you post once a day on most of the sites you are active on to ensure that you can engage with your social media audience.

⟡ **Examples of active social media efforts:**

We can all find inspiration from organizations that are innovative when it comes to social media. Here are some case studies:

Kentucky Fried Chicken – KFC[33] conducted an exciting campaign on X. They followed 11 people on X – *Five Spice Girls and Six Guys Named Herb*. This generated widespread interest among fans curious why KFC did this. The campaign was outed by @edgette22 when he tweeted the following post:

"Eleven Herbs and spices are what is included in KFC's secret recipe!"

KFC tweeted that @Edgette22 was "one smart fella."

Other companies use YouTube videos to build awareness and recognition for their product or service. With YouTube videos, companies can get consumers involved in their brand and create brand advocates. For example, Blendtec,[34] a blending appliance company, has a series of online commercials called, "Will it Blend?" The CEO inserts objects such as a rake, a Rubik's cube, marbles, and even an iPhone into a blender to see what happens. According to management, these YouTube videos helped increase sales for the mixer by 700%.

Another interesting approach was one that the UK firm, Companies House,[35] conducted. They produced a series of business videos on YouTube that featured innovative companies. Reach Robotics, one of the firms represented by Companies House, used robotics, gaming, and Augmented

Reality to entertain and inspire people. In a video, Silas Adekunle, Reach Robotics CEO, discussed his background, vision and reasons why he created Reach Robotics.

👍 My Observation...

Small businesses can thrive using social media, but they must strategize and develop a plan before embarking on a social media marketing plan. It takes time, a lot of time, to reap the benefits. If you don't have the time, hire someone.

The biggest obstacle to launching and implementing a social media marketing plan is money. I always tell my clients that you need to spend money to make money. Don't be short-sighted. Allocate resources and make sure you follow through with your plan. Doing so will help you thrive.

The social media marketing plan should be included in the integrated marketing plan under the tactics section. Read the pages that follow to see which relevant sites target your market.

BLOG

BLOGS AND MICROBLOGS

"For me, my blog came before social media. I started writing little journals about my family and just kept them there. Over the years, I built a following and then eventually started sharing those same blog posts on social media. But the core of my readers click directly on my blog. I think a blog is a great place for brands to utilize when wanting to share more about their brands and give a more in-depth look into the story behind them." Brianne Manz, Owner, Stroller In The City, www.strollerinthecity.com, NYC

At this point, a blog is almost as standard as a newspaper.[36] In 2009, when I wrote my first book, **Everything You Ever Wanted to Know About Social Media, but were afraid to ask...**, very few people were reading blogs, let alone understanding what they were.

A blog can help you build a presence in a crowded marketplace. It's written informally as if you were speaking with someone. It can delve into topics about travel, media, parenthood, weight-loss, fitness, and so much more.

I started my blog in March 2008. I have hundreds of posts about everything from current clients, to annoying situations, to family matters, staffing issues, running a small business, travel, wine, health, and more.

When my blog was nominated as a finalist in the 2008 Stevie Awards for Women in Business as the Blog of the Year, it helped me gain recognition from industry leaders, some of whom are now clients. To make the site more exciting and appealing to a wide range of people, I accept guest bloggers. But my reach extends beyond blogs to my radio podcast, Hilary Topper on Air.

On my podcast, I specifically gear it for the small business owner who wants to grow both personally and professionally. I interview businesspeople and experts in the health and fitness area. Sometimes the content overlaps but I find that there's an audience who likes to listen to content as opposed to read it. New shows air once a week, so be sure to tune in.

○ History of the Blog

When teaching at Hofstra, before I talk about why people should blog or what they should blog about, I often tell my students about the history of the blog.[37] To me, it puts things in perspective. Here is a rundown:

- 1994, a Swarthmore student, Justin Hall, created the first blog, Links.net.
- December 1997, Jorn Barger, an online "blogger" coins the term "weblog" for "logging the web."
- April 1999, a programmer Peter Merholz, shortens Weblog to blog.
- December 2002, the gossip blog, Gawker launches.

- June 2003, Google launches Adsense to put ads on blogs.
- June 2004, Merriam Webster declares "blog" word of the year.
- January 2005, 32 million Americans read blogs.
- May 2005, Huffington Post launches.
- October 2019, there are more than 19.4 billion blogs on WordPress.

⟡ Why Blog?

My husband thinks it is crazy to let people know so much information about you. By blogging, he believes, you are putting yourself in jeopardy and undermining your security.

Perhaps he has a point. Therefore, I am mindful about my blog and what information I make available. The thousands of people reading my blogs are potential customers.

Through my blog, I want to let these potential customers know that I am an honest businesswoman with a lot of integrity. They can gain insights into the way I conduct myself in a more personal way and establish a deeper connection then if we first met, say, over email, or even through an introduction. As we all know, people do business with people they like.

My blog is the first step for would-be clients and collaborators to get to know the type of person I am and the way I run my business. Hopefully, they like me and will want to learn more about the ways in which my staff and I can help them. The blog also increases the search engine optimization (SEO) for me as chief executive officer of HJMT and the company's website, which has garnered new leads for potential clients.

♻ Increasing Your SEO

Besides utilizing my blog to link back to my company website, I also help increase the SEO for my actual blog by linking to things that I talk about in my blog entries. For example, if I discuss Enterprise Rent-A-Car, I will link the firm's name to its corporate website. Every time I mention a company name, I link to its website. Also, you can "tag" several different keywords as well. These words are used as meta tags, which is HTML code, that often appears on the website's backend and every time they come up on the internet, they will link to other places that it appears.

There are several plugins that you can use with WordPress that enable you to have keyword-friendly copy in both the headline and the body copy. My favorite is called Yoast, because it helps you make your copy SEO ready.

Another way to increase your SEO is inputting the most relevant keywords. These keywords can be found through Google WebMaster Tools. Google Webmaster Tools tie in with your Google Analytics report and provide you with the right words to use on your blog, or any other online site for that matter, to increase your SEO. For more detailed information, see the chapter on SEO.

♻ Where to Blog

So, you want to blog, but don't know how to do it? There are several different services on the web that are free to use, including seven of the top blogging sites including their pros and cons. Take this information and make a decision as to what platform you want to use for your blog.

☝ **Here are the pros and cons of each:**

Blogger (BlogSpot)

Pro: Free and easy to use. Con: Limiting, and Google owns your content.

Example: https://www.renewpilates.com/

Tumblr

Pro: Free and easy to use; integrates well with social media and you can add images and video easily. Con: Limited features and backup is cumbersome.

Example: http://willitbeard.com/

Squarespace

Pro: Simple to use; professional; e-commerce available. Con: Can only include 20 pages on a website and two contributors (as of the publishing of this book); otherwise there's a fee.

Example: http://www.eggshopnyc.com/

Wix

Pro: Dozens of templates and third-party apps; quick set up. Con: Free account is limited. Custom templates available for $4.50 a month.

Example: https://maapilim.com/

WordPress

Pro: Easy to use and manage. Con: Limited options. You can't have ads, and you don't own the blog.

Example: http://chicago.suntimes.com/

WordPress.org

Pro: 45,000+ plugins and SEO friendly. Con: Learning curve, and you need to back up and manage security.

Example: http://www.travelportland.com

Weebly

Pro: Easy to use with a drag-and-drop format. Con: Limited features and exporting is difficult.

Example: http://www.douksnow.com/

If you are going to embark on a blog, consider using WordPress. Despite its learning curve, WordPress is easy to use, and most blogs and websites are created through this program. Here, you can purchase a template or get a free template and customize the site to suit your needs.

WordPress enables you to do more with the blog with plugins and advanced customization tools. Most media outlets use WordPress so that they can easily update and customize the blog.

The other consideration to factor into your decision on a blogging platform is content and ownership rights. According to the blog site, "Search for Blogging,"[38] because Google owns

Blogger, it owns your content. On the other hand, you own your content with WordPress. Many designers work with WordPress and can easily set you up with a customized blog for a nominal design fee.

⚬ How to Set Up a Blog

Start by going to GoDaddy or Network Solutions and purchase a URL that is unique to your brand or business. You can have your site hosted there, or consider another third-party provider. There are tons of hosting companies. This is where your website will live. Also determine whether your site will be backed up on the cloud or internal server. We use a company called WPEngine, a Google company to host our site. It also backs up our site every day.

⚬ Characteristics of a Great Blog or Website

A great blog or website is easy to navigate, and visitors can always get back to the homepage, no matter where they are on the site. The URL is easy to remember. Images load quickly, and the website is responsive (meaning, it's mobile-friendly).

When it comes to the homepage, make sure some element – text or an image – changes somewhere on the page—whether it's a blog, a X feed or something so that the SEO aggregates appropriately each day.

When clients embark on a new website or blog site, I suggest that they start with a web map. This is a plan that lays out where you will put all of your content and images. With a web map, start with the homepage and then plan out several tabs – perhaps an "About Us," a "Services" or a "Resource" tab. It's up to you. Then think about other categories that fall within those tabs.

With a WordPress website, you can find free templates here:

- MyThemeshop.com
- Wpexplorer.com
- Fabthemes.com

It's essential to think about the site's visual appeal. Does the color reflect the mood or the brand? Are you using high-quality images and graphics? Is the text large enough to read? Is there enough white space?

Look at other websites that draw your interest and emulate them – but do not copy them. Instead, get inspired by these websites to help you determine what you like and which direction to pursue going forward.

If you decide to use WordPress, here are some of my favorite plugins:

- **Contact Form 7** – Enables you to get data by providing a contact form for someone looking to do business with you.
- **Yoast** – Helps boost SEO by providing suggestions for keywords and meta tags.
- **WooCommerce** – Facilitates e-commerce.
- **Google Analytics** – Provides real data on your audience.
- **Disqus** – Offers a comment platform.
- **MailChimp for WordPress** – Provides a marketing platform for your business, with provisions for e-mail

and social media campaigns and data analytics. I use MailChimp all the time, and this integration works like a gem.

- **WordFence or Better WP Security** – Protects your site from hackers.
- **Updraft** – Backs up the site.
- **Elementor** – Drag-and-drop website builder for WordPress.

ᗑ A Word About Security

If you launch a website, make sure you create a secure username. Don't use the default "admin." Also, the best passwords feature numbers, capitals, and characters, offering the best protection against hackers.

Make a periodic backup of your WordPress database and be sure to update to WordPress' latest version. You may consider using a security plugin to monitor your activity as well. This will help you keep your site safe and protected.

ᗑ How Do You Determine if Blogging is For You?

Many companies have company blog posts. You may also want an individual blog. Whatever you decide, blogs are an effective way to get your message out and increase your SEO. If you want to determine whether or not to blog, ask yourself, "do I have the content and do I have the time?"

✋ Your First Post

So, you've decided that blogging is for you. You visit WordPress or Blogger and create a blog. What's next? What do you write about?

The first post should be an introduction. Tell the reader who you are and why you're writing. Also, give your readers an overview of what the blog will be about. After that, blog often. Don't blog once and not blog again for a week or two or even three. I know some folks who have blogs and have not updated them in months. The more you update, the more people will follow your posts. If you don't update your blog regularly, then readers will lose interest, and the few times you do post will be a waste of time.

My first post on NYLifestyleBlog.com introduced my firm. My second post was this:

> *"Hey, does anyone out there know what the proper etiquette is for picking up the tab when you have a business lunch? I ask because I attend business lunches almost every day. I meet with clients. I meet with prospects. I meet with business friends. I always thought the rule of thumb was, if I'm "pitching" something, I should pay. If the other party is trying to "pitch" me, they pay. If no one is selling, you split the tab.*
>
> *Sound right?*
>
> *Well, recently I went to breakfast with someone who's been trying to get together for a long time. We talked a bit about his business and about mine. He tried to sell me a sponsorship for one of his upcoming endeavors.*

*When the waitress came by, he ordered an egg omelet. I
ordered a single egg. I didn't think about who would pay
for what until the bill came. It was $22 for breakfast.
He quickly took the bill and put it on his side. I politely
asked him how much I owe, and he told me $11.*

*I started to think should I have not said anything and let him
pick up the tab? Should I grab the bill and insist on paying?
I made the conscience decision to split the bill. But all I kept
thinking was "Why should I pay $11 for a single egg?"*

*Later in the day, I went for lunch with a retired client.
Since she no longer works, my thought was I was paying
for lunch. When the bill came, she quickly grabbed it
and when I asked how much, she said it was on her.
That surprised me since I invited her and she's no
longer employed. I graciously accepted the lunch and
thought, whoever pays, it all evens out at the end."*

This post set the tone for all subsequent blogs. It was written
in a casual way and opened the door to conversation. I
received a lot of feedback and met new clients. Blogging has
certainly helped me gain business.

☼ Pick a Theme

Blog about a specific topic. For example, some people blog
about business-related issues, an approach favored by Seth
Godin,[39] author of **Tribes** and **Purple Cow**. Others blog about
travel, lifestyle, entertainment, skiing, parenting, or even the
challenges of a small business owner. No matter what the
theme, stick with it, and use that niche to your advantage to

help you sharpen your persona as an expert in your particular field.

When choosing, pick a theme that you love. It can correlate with your business, or it could be about something else. Whatever your decision, make sure you have enough content to post at least once or twice a week.

How Will People Find You?

People will find you through WordPress or Blogger. They will also find you through search engines with keywords. For example, if someone is looking for a recommendation on a hotel in Cancun, and your blog focuses on travel, your blog may come up in the search engine results page.

Also, consider marketing your blog. Tell everyone you have a blog. Make sure that people know when there is a new post and new information so that they know the blog is timely.

When I have a new post, I have an RSS feed that alerts my subscribers. I microblog and send a link to my online community via my social network. I also include my blog in my signature line in all of my emails. By doing this, I pick up new readers with every entry.

Blog Comments

Are you able to monitor comments? Of course. You will receive an email that enables you to see and approve each new blog comment. If you would like to reject the comment because it may be offensive or irrelevant, you can do so on the blogging platform, and the comment will never make it to the post – so no one will see it. If you accept the comment, it will appear within the post.

I use the Disqus plugin on my blog. Disqus enables the members of my community to comment, and they see my responses on my blog. I've been using this for years, and it works well.

✋ Content Creation/Microblogging

Since X is 280 characters, I like to use that as my base on many of the different sites, except Instagram, where I would create more content.

Today, the most effective microblogs capture the readers' attention instantaneously and bring those readers to the link to your site.

Here are some microblogs that I recently posted:

- Interesting news from #AugmentedReality eyewear, @vuzix - http://bit.ly/2qE4Jsw
- Want to learn to swim faster in the pool? http://bit.ly/2r9dX3v.
- Do you feel like you keep getting injured or an old injury doesn't go away?
- http://bit.ly/2qEg5fX.
- This is my favorite place to #run - http://bit.ly/2qE9UIT.

✋ What Makes a Compelling Post?

There are different types of posts that attract consumers including:

- Humorous posts that make people laugh.
- Tips or something that your community will find helpful.
- Tell a good story. Storytelling is key in content creation.
- Make the post visually appealing.

When writing posts, think about what would grab your buyer persona's attention.

When using X or any other microblogging tool, check for readers' replies to your questions and your direct responses (or DM). You will be surprised how many people will answer your questions or even link to your blog!

Microblog about happenings at your organization several times a day. Examples can include:

- "Did you know that at @HJMT we recently received an Emmy for a client video?"
- "Did you watch our YouTube videos on how to create an integrated marketing plan? Here's the link: http://bit.ly/31GfRaN.

Remember to be conversational, hence conversational media, in tone and post things that people will find interesting. Also, don't be shy about getting involved in dialogues with those who reach out to you in response to your postings. The more discussions you have with your community, the more people will be engaged.

✍ Using Blogs to Promote Your Product or Service

In addition to your blog, consider either guest blogging on another site or having bloggers write about your product or service to give you more exposure and visibility.

Many restaurant owners invite bloggers to write restaurant reviews for them. They contact the bloggers, offer them a "free dinner" in exchange for a write-up, and the bloggers post about the restaurant, service, and food. These bloggers publish their reviews and then share with their community. For example, if you have 10 bloggers writing about your restaurant and they have a following of at least 100 people each, more than 1,000 people will read about your restaurant. Then those 1,000 people share the blog with their friends, and now 2,000 people will learn about you. If you ask the blogger to also post on Google and Yelp and they do, you have a home run.

Other businesses invite bloggers to review their products and services as well. Authors, new product introductions, facilities, and even dental offices work with bloggers to promote their business.

Pay-per-blog is a service where bloggers are paid to write about a subject matter. If you are a shoe company, for example, and want people to review your shoes, you may go on a pay-per-blog site and ask people to write about your product. By clicking on "pay-per-blog" in a Google search, you will find numerous sites that will pay bloggers to post on their behalf.

Years ago, the power belonged in the hands of the media. Today, it's the bloggers and consumers that influence what we eat, what we drink, where we go for fun, and what we do on a Saturday evening.

Blogging is the ultimate word of mouth marketing technique. One recommendation leads to another, and before you know it, dozens, hundreds, thousands, or even millions of people hear about something all through viral marketing. But remember, bloggers should always be honest and authentic with their posts.

Transparency is key. Don't always blog about the same thing either. Variety is a necessity! Whenever I blog about personal topics, I get many more responses than when I blog about business. However, I know that people do read the business content because they always mention something about a past blog post when I see them, or they write about it on a social networking site.

☝ Viewing Your Stats

On every blogging application, you can monitor or track how many people are looking at your blog. Many of these programs will enable you to see which post was the most popular and which was least popular.

On Blogger, for example, you can install a counter to see how many people have visited your site. Counters are free and can come from Google Analytics, FreeStats, Easy Hit Counter, or StatCounter.

On WordPress.com, a free stat counter is included in the site. To install it, use your WordPress.com API key sent to you when you sign up. Once the counter is installed, it begins running and collecting information about the blogger's page views, the most popular posts, where blog traffic is coming from, and what people click on when they leave. It also adds a link to your dashboard so you can see your blog's stats on one page.

I still like using Google Analytics and Page Analytics for that. It reinforces which blog post works, which doesn't and tells me what my community wants to hear more of in terms of content.

👍 **My Observation...**

Although many may say blogging is dying, I don't agree. I think blogging is very much alive and can help you build your brand. Blogging is essential for almost any business. Pitch bloggers and see if they would review your product or service. If they do, you will have some active backlinks to your site. If you want to be a thought-leader in a particular industry, consider guest blogging on an established site on your topic of expertise to get your name out.

Now, look at your integrated marketing plan. Does a blog make sense for you? If so, add to your plan.

BUILDING AN AMBASSADOR PROGRAM

"Brands of all sizes can benefit from working with influencers. Influencers give brands an opportunity to tap into already established audiences, receive beautiful content that can be repurposed across omnichannels and have access to influential voices who can inspire action. The influencer space is growing every day and is not slowing down. As the space expands, influencers will be looking for longer-term partnerships, similar to celebrity talent, to create an authentic, believable storyline for their fans and have dedicated relationships in a particular product category. When working with influencers, it's important to remember that not all influencers can work for every program or meet every objective. Depending on the follower size of the influencer, they can serve different functions – mega influencers are strong awareness and relevance drivers whereas micro influencers can help with engagement and conversion. Based on brand priorities, I always recommend working with a mix of both to meet a variety of needs." Zoey Topper, Senior Manager, Weber Shandwick, NYC

The term "influencer" is hot these days. Most smart brands seek out those who have ample followers on either Instagram, Snapchat, a blog, YouTube, or any other social networking site. They do this because they know if an influencer endorses their product or service, this will generate more awareness and purchases.

Bloggers, who are also considered influencers, have a powerful voice. According to marketing guru Jeff Bullas,[40] "blogging doesn't make you an expert, but just through the sheer commitment, research involved and the passion required to write often and regularly, the expert label perceived or real starts to shine through." BlogHer,[41] the leading conference for women bloggers, says 81% trust bloggers and 61% purchased something as a result of a blog post.

☝ What Is The Difference Between Ambassadors, Influencers and Bloggers?

Ambassadors, influencers and bloggers essentially are all the same in that they have a large group of followers who trust and respect them. Most people use the word, "influencer" to describe anyone who has a significant following. Their audience listens to what they say and/or suggest. Listed below are the differences.

- **Brand ambassador** is a person you select for a long-term assignment to help you build brand awareness. They either get paid by the brand or receive swag in return for payment.
- **An influencer** is used by a brand for a shorter assignment and they typically get paid.

- **Bloggers** can have a short-term assignment. For example, a brand may pitch a blogger to review a product or service. Or, they may recruit a blogger for a long-term assignment. These long-term projects are often paid opportunities.

Influencers are not created equally. There are nano-influencers who have less than 1,000 followers on Instagram (or any other social media site) but get great engagement. Micro-influencers who have followers in excess of 10,000 people. Then there are macro-influencers with 100,000 – 1 million followers and mega-influencers with 1,000,000 and up followers.

If you utilize influencers with such large numbers, make sure they have real followers and also don't be surprised by the sticker price of single post. You might pay $20,000 for a single post to an influencer with more than 1 million followers.

Instagram has led to the rise of influencers because content is seen more readily and there's a lot of engagement on the site. Since that is the case, most influencers are on Instagram.

One of the most prominent places for setting up brand ambassadors is in the sports fields. Companies that produce sports drinks, bike racks, triathlon clothing, socks, sneakers, you name it, if the company markets to athletes, it has brand ambassadors.

The exciting part about brand ambassadors is that you don't always have to pay them with cash. But you do need to give them product. I was particularly impressed with a company called Balega International. They make running socks. The socks are well-made and produced in South Africa.

The group selected a few dozen "ambassadors" and asked them to share the love of their socks on their blogs and on social media. When they broached the subject of having an ambassador program, I jumped at the opportunity, and I am now a brand ambassador for the company. When I first started Team Galloway LI, a Long Island running club, the company provided a pair of socks to each of the members of my club. They also provided six pairs of socks to the WeRTriathletes team, a virtual triathlon team. Everyone was thrilled, and they created dozens of additional ambassadors that tell everyone about their socks. Good deal. Right?

☝ How To Set Up An Ambassador Program

Start by determining your goals and figuring out who should be an ambassador. Then create a plan of action for the ambassadors. What should they do for you? Here are some possibilities.

- Create content on their social channels or blogs.
- Share messages that they can post regarding your brand.
- Answer questions from a frequently asked questions fact sheet that you can provide to your ambassadors which they can share with their community.
- Create buzz by offering your influencers a series of intriguing posts about your brand.

Make sure ambassadors get something in return for helping you. Then, measure the success of the program. How much was posted? How big were their communities? How much reach did they have? How much traffic did you get to your website as a result of their efforts? What was your ROI (Return on Investment)?

To connect with influencers, look at Cision, Google, X, Snapchat, Instagram, Facebook or any other site that you feel targets your buyer persona. Check out what they write about, what they do on social sites and how involved their followers are with them. Once you do your homework, look at their engagement as well to determine if they are the right fit for your brand. It's important to look at their likes and comments before you choose them to represent you as an influencer.

Target bloggers by sending them an introductory pitch letter and offer a sample of your product. Invite them to events and exclusive opportunities. Try to make them feel special and keep in touch often.

By including blog ambassadors into your organization, they will become part of your corporate family and when they feel connected, they want to do more for you.

⚙ Experiences With Various Brands

With more than 1 million followers on social, my blogs and my podcast, I'm accurately described as an influencer. I've been active in the digital world since 2006, and my community perpetually grows. Many have larger communities than I do, but what sets me apart, is I've worked on both sides. Major brands have pitched me to become a brand ambassador, and I've pitched bloggers to help brands I represent connect to their target market.

Here are some of the brands I've worked with and what they did right. I hope this helps you in determining if hiring an influencer is right for you.

Google Glass Explorer:

To read the case study, refer to the Google Glass Sidebar.

What the company did right:

- Google Glass provided a private community where explorers could network and be part of something bigger than themselves.
- They built communities on Google Plus, which were very active, and Google Glass explorers became instant friends with each other, cross promoting each other's activities on social.
- They had one person who curated the group and brought the group to another level.
- After Google Glass successfully used influencers, other brands followed in a big way.

Balega International:

As I previously mentioned, I became involved with Balega International a few years ago. The makers of running socks, Balega had a great group of ambassadors who love their socks. As an ambassador, I received a box filled with socks and other items to use while running, and, in return, I have recorded videos, posted content and blogged about the socks. Along with that, every month, I posted at least twice using the hashtag #balegalove or just #balega.

What the company did right:

- Balega brought the ambassadors into their world by providing contests every month and making the ambassadors feel wanted and part of the team. They had an active Facebook page, and they send out monthly newsletters with new contests and activation ideas.

Instavit

Not all companies have a great brand ambassador program. Instavit makes vitamins that are easy to swallow because they are sprayable. You spray in your mouth, and you get the benefits of your daily vitamin intake.

When they put out a call for ambassadors, the company selected me as one of them for my health and wellness blog. I accepted. I loved the idea of a sprayable vitamin because I have a hard time swallowing pills.

They sent me a package. I reviewed the product on my blog, and the company put my photo up on their website. And then nothing. The company never reached back out. I tweeted and re-tweeted various tweets that included the company, and they never said anything. When I asked for more product, the company said it would send it out, but then I never received it.

This non-responsiveness did not keep me engaged. I liked the product, but the ambassador program person never followed up.

What the company did right:

- The company recruited the right ambassadors with the right buyer persona for its brand.

Headsweats

Headsweats, a cap company, reached out to me, asking if I would be interested in its brand ambassador program. Because I already knew the brand and already had a couple of its running caps, I was excited to be part of the experience.

I was asked along with at least 100 other ambassadors to be included in the program. The other ambassadors were included in one of the following 10 categories including triathlon, running, cycling, endurance running, fitness, hiking, water sports, snowboarding, and trail running.

We were asked to post on social at least once a month and share information about Headsweats to our community. In return, Headsweats provided the ambassadors with a private community for networking and mailed out four packages a year of at least two caps plus other swag items.

What the company did right:

- By selecting dozens of people in each category, Headsweats increased its chances of getting publicity and building awareness for the brand.
- The company looked at its buyer persona and determined that the categories it selected were the perfect place to start in its campaign.
- Headsweats welcomed its ambassadors with open arms and re-tweeted their tweets on an ongoing basis.

☝ Blogger Outreach:

I get a ton of pitch letters from public relations firms. Most send me information and have never looked at my blog or know what I write about. It is essential to research each blog before you pitch to the blogger.

The other thing I noticed, many publicists that pitch me have little to no follow up skills. In my PR business, we follow up at least five times. Follow up is imperative in getting your story placed, especially on a blog.

☝ Do's and Don'ts for Building an Ambassador/Influencer Program

Do:

- Research your community and find the influencers that you think will rally behind you and promote your brand.
- Stay in contact with them and develop a relationship. Don't just pitch once. If the influencer uses your product, don't forget about them. Maintain the relationship.
- Keep the ambassadors in a program connected with you and with each other.
- Make them feel like they're part of your family.
- Find someone who can spearhead the leadership process.
- Create a community for ambassadors on Facebook in a private group.
- Send them information on an ongoing basis.

- Ask them to pitch ideas to you that could generate significant interest, as Balega and Headsweats did.
- Show them love because that love will come back twofold.
- Remember that the personal touch works. Reach out and develop a relationship with the influencer.

Don't:

- Send anything irrelevant to an influencer.
- Not respond!
- Promise and not deliver.

An active influencer program can turn your product into a success. It can also help you build brand awareness to your target market.

♥ How to Choose the Right Influencer for Your Brand

Before embarking on a brand ambassador program, ask yourself, "Who is it that I want to target?" Think about your "buyer persona" and create a profile for that person.

Listed below are some guidelines for choosing the right ambassador for your brand:

- How old is the person? Is he or she a millennial? A baby boomer? A senior?
- Is this person a woman, man, transgender, gender-neutral?
- What does the person do for a living?
- Where does the person live?
- Does this person live in a house? Apartment?
- What motivates the potential ambassador?
- What are some of the ambassador's goals or aspirations?
- Why does that person want to be an ambassador?
- How big is that person's social reach? Blog? YouTube reach?
- Does the person's blog correlate to your brand?
- What are their audience demographics?
- What do they post about?
- Do they already post about topics that relate to your brand?
- Do they have interests/passions that align with your brand?
- Do they represent diversity?

☝ **My Observation...**

If you get an influencer to help spread the word out about your brand, you will likely see an increase in traffic to your blog and website. Make sure to get the right ratio between what you offer vs. what you get back so that you get as much exposure and visibility as possible.

Go back to your integrated marketing plan. If you want to attract influencers for your brand, make sure you include a summary in the tactic section of your integrated marketing plan.

SOCIAL NETWORKING SITES

"Not all posts will inspire you, but all you need is to inspire one, to make a difference for a person," Noah Lam, Head Coach, Lightning Warriors Youth Triathlon Team, Long Island, NY

In the following pages, you will learn what various social networking sites are, how to use them, and the demographics of each. This should help you determine whether or not to include them in your integrated marketing plan.

W'SUP FACEBOOK! WHO ISN'T ON FACEBOOK?

"It broke my heart that Russian bots targeting specific populations in swing state areas of our country with memes and ads on Facebook directly affected the outcome of our presidential election, thereby undermining our American democracy. The idealism of social media as a unifier of the world was in a master stroke perverted to hatred and greed ... this is a huge lesson for media developers." Jeris Jill Huntington, Huntington Universal, WA

Facebook is a social networking platform where you can join networks organized by region, city, workplace, school, families, product, venue or cause, and where you can connect and interact with other people. If you have ever seen the movie, The Social Network,[42] you know the origin of this website was to connect students with other students from Harvard University; then it was opened to other universities. In the early 2000s, Facebook became mainstream. Today, anyone can make a Facebook account, and there are more than 2.41 billion users on Facebook.[43] The networking site continuously grows and adds new products to monetize itself.

Besides allowing you to connect and interact with people from all over the world, Facebook is popular because you can share interests, events, and news on both a personal and business level. Though the way people use Facebook is continually evolving, investing in a presence on Facebook should be a priority in both marketing your business and building your online community.

Facebook is a great place to promote my blogs and podcasts. It enables me to share with my 5,000+ friends and followers. It also enables me to create subgroups of various topics.

For example, I have various Facebook groups, including NY Lifestyle Blog, Triathlete's Diary, WeRTriathletes, Team Galloway LI, Hilary Topper on Air, and the list goes on. Within each group, I try to create conversations and offer suggestions or share articles from my blog.

Why is Facebook so popular? The thing about Facebook is, there is very little learning curve. It's easy to use and people see that all their friends and family are on the site, so they readily jump on.

♨ Connecting on Facebook

There are endless possibilities with whom you can connect with on Facebook, and your world may become richer because of it.

♨ Former Employees

It's essential to keep up with former employees, especially those who parted ways on good terms. You never know if they will become future clients or even employees again. I keep up with several of my former employees. They were very dedicated, and I am genuinely interested in what they are doing. Other benefits include sharing potential referral sources, and information such as future networking events.

☝ Future Employees

Facebook is a great way to check out someone's background. If privacy settings permit, you get an opportunity to view photos, check out their friends, and even get a sense of their interests. This enables me to determine if these potential employees are a good fit with my current staff. I also love connecting with my students and following their careers. Hey, you never know, I may end up retaining their services or even hiring them.

At a business lunch the other day, an attorney friend told me that he only hires staff with whom he would break bread. Facebook allows you to see your potential employees' interests. However, if they keep their profile private, you won't be able to access anything, and that may signify a red flag.

☝ Deeper Understanding of Established Clients

People want to do business with people they like. That is a fact. The more you know about your clients, the more you can share common ground and cultivate a relationship that goes deeper than just business services.

Facebook enables members to learn about compelling aspects of people's lives. Participants frequently update their status line. Sometimes people use the platform to share what they are doing. Other times they post about a situation, a problem, a call for resources, a link to their blog, or an informative post.

☺ Developing New Relationships with Potential Clients

Another way to use Facebook is to create new relationships with potential clients. Here, if they are the type that shares information, you find out their interests and details about their families. It allows you to make a deeper connection with them and builds lasting bonds. Social media is all about relationship building, and Facebook will enable you to do just that.

Though my established clients have invited me to be their Facebook friends, I have also met potential clients on Facebook because my activity on the platform resonates, allowing me to dialogue with new people. I consistently update my status. I also join groups and comment on the status of others by offering advice, congratulating them on the news they post or sharing an upbeat sentiment.

☺ Personalizing Your Profile

Your profile is the place to list your likes, dislikes, music preferences, and favorite movies. It is where you describe how you earn your living and talk about past positions, the schools you attended and more. There is the opportunity to post a great deal of information in this section, and you should try to utilize it. Through your profile, people will get to know you better, and the more people know you, the more they will relate to you and want to do business with you.

☝ The Profile Photo

On Facebook, you can post a photo or an avatar (a character or an image). What does this photo say about you? I like to use a picture that is fun and shows who I am. It could be a photo of me at a race or it could be a photo of me exploring the world. Whatever photo I chose, I try to change up the image every month to build engagement.

While it is okay to use family or personal photos, be careful not to post a photo that you may not want everyone – including a potential client or employer – to see.

☝ Privacy Settings

Many people ask me if there is a privacy setting on Facebook, and the answer is yes. There are different levels of privacy. You can permit the entire Facebook community to see your information. Alternatively, you can allow limited details to be public or make your Facebook page private so that no one sees it unless they are friends. I recommend keeping the profile public if you are using Facebook for business development. This way, more people will see your information.

Now, if you want a private group, you can create a separate Facebook group for just your family where you can post photos and discuss family related topics. In my family, my sister-in-law, Sharon, created the Topper Family group, where we share personal information and no one but the invited guests can see what is included.

Today, there are many security issues regarding privacy including harassment and stalkers. For these reasons, some may choose to make their Facebook private and just communicate solely with family and friends. However, if you are using Facebook for business purposes, it's important to keep your profile public.

☼ Features on Facebook

To understand the power of Facebook, you will need to learn about its various elements. Listed below are some of the necessary foundations:

☼ Your Newsfeed

The newsfeed features a status line, where your friends can leave comments. Your friends can even ask you questions and carry on a conversation. If there is one thing to remember, it's this: The newsfeed is not a private conversation, other Facebook members can see what you write on your wall.

For example, in a post I made as a joke to a friend, I wrote that I took a photograph while driving and ended the post by saying, "but don't tell anyone!" This spurred many conversations, including a friend who is a police officer telling me to pull over.

☝ Finding Friends

To grow your community, start with the search feature. Enter your high school and put in your graduating year. You will be surprised how many people who graduated with you are on Facebook. Also, search for the year you graduated from college, places where you worked, current employment. Once you have five to 10 friends, look at their Facebook friends who appear on their profile page. More than likely, you will find many people you know.

☝ Photo Albums

The photo album is a great vehicle to promote past and current events, product launches, and even internal meetings. Photos can be uploaded on Facebook, and whenever you add new images, the newsfeed posts updates for all of your friends to see. Some of the privacy settings limit what people can see.

☝ Events

Through the Facebook event feature, you can get exposure and visibility for your upcoming social or business gatherings. Many people use this feature for business networking groups, while others use it for fundraisers. These events help you keep your community involved in what you are doing. Also, while it is tempting to invite everyone you know to an event, it is important to target only those who would be interested in receiving these notifications. Otherwise, your Facebook friends may see you as a nuisance and dismiss your future updates and invitations.

ⵔ **Pages**

At HJMT, we advise our clients to create a business page. On this page, you can create posts that acknowledge new clients, new employees, new sponsors, and even company milestones. Try to post at least three to five times a week on this page. However, beware, that even though you may build this page to have numerous followers, not many people will see your actual posts in their newsfeeds unless you "boost" them with paid advertising dollars. This is how Facebook makes money! In the digital advertising chapter, we talk about digital ads but Facebook ads don't have to cost a lot. You can boost a post for $20 and have 10,000+ people see the post.

To move away from the page and offer added value to your customers and potential customers, we recommend creating a group. This is a great way to build engagement. However, you need to allocate a moderator who can generate content and respond to questions posted in the group.

We also recommend you consider joining some of the numerous groups that are relevant to your organization; these groups can include golf, music, animals, business, social media, journalism, and more. There an array of groups ranging from skiers to people who have children with disabilities. There is even a group for caretakers of people with dementia. Everyone seems to be on Facebook. Even if they don't post, they are still reading your posts. This is another vehicle from which to target a niche community, especially if you have a product or service that suits their needs.

☝ Groups

There are three types of groups – secret, closed and public. The secret groups are great if you have a team of people you want to communicate with privately. The closed groups are non-searchable to those who aren't members. On a public group, everyone on Facebook has the opportunity to see the group and its content.

☝ Video

In subsequent chapters, I will cover YouTube and other video sites, but Facebook also enables users to upload videos and livestream. Videos can serve as great marketing tools because there are many consumers who are visual buyers. Here you can showcase your business.

Livestreaming is popular. Everyone wants to show the world where they are and what's transpiring at a given moment. Through Facebook Live, you can share your view of the world with your community.

☝ Status

Most social networking sites have a status line. This line tells your community what you are currently doing. I like to use the status line to spread the word about my blog entries, events that we are promoting, and even publicity opportunities or new product introductions. Throughout the day, I update my status so that my community sees what I am up to.

♨ Tips for Good Status Updates

Keep your status updates upbeat, not too personal, not desperate, and not too revealing. You want the status to leave people with a positive impression of you. All too often, people pour their heart out on Facebook. This is something you should be aware of. I'm to blame here also. I've done it dozens of times, but if you want to keep more of a private life, don't post it on Facebook.

♨ Mobile Phone

I like mobile integration. Many sites offer this feature, but Facebook makes mobile integration particularly easy. Every time you get a new message, you see it immediately on your iPhone or Android.

♨ Marketplace

Facebook enables you and your company to advertise similar to Craigslist. If you own a second-hand thrift shop, antique jewelry shop, or you are a home organizer, this may be a perfect place for you to do business. Here you can post photos of things you are selling and on the flip side, you may want to go here for things you may need.

♨ Facebook Advertising

Advertisers can potentially get tens of thousands of hits a day. This is different than a boosted post. This is a display ad that appears on a targeted newsfeed. However, each hit means the advertiser must ante up a fee to Facebook. This could be very costly, especially when people are randomly clicking a link and have no interest in the company's product or service.

The other day, I was researching a dentist who recently purchased a massive amount of equipment for his office. He was considering promoting his services through online sources. I noticed that one of his competitors was on Facebook, so I clicked on the link and snooped around. Interestingly, this competitor's ad campaign had a relatively long run, which suggested that his advertising dollars worked on Facebook.

☼ Facebook Stories and Reels

Since Facebook acquired Instagram, they have been trying to use some of the tools that work in Instagram on Facebook, including Facebook Stories and Reels. Here, you can generate a story or you can use your status update in the story so that more people will see it. I utilize stories and Reels when I want to promote something including my blogs.

☼ Demographics of Facebook Users

According to Omnicore Agency,[44]

- There are more than 2.96 billion active monthly users.
- 53% are female and 47% are male.
- 82% are college educated.
- Majority of the users are between 50 and up.

♥ The Psychology of a Like: Survey Shows What People Like on Facebook

If you're like me, you probably post often and then wonder why people "like" or don't acknowledge or comment on specific posts. It's been a source of curiosity for me for the past few years. So, in conjunction with HJMT Public Relations, I decided to poll our social communities.

Our first question was, "Do you post on Facebook?" Many people on Facebook don't post at all while others seem to post multiple times a day. Of the nearly 200 people surveyed from across the country, 70% said they only post when they have something important to say. Only 10% said they post every day, and almost 20% said they don't post at all.

Of those who use Facebook, 78% said they like something when they see a friend or family member's accomplishment. And 53% said that inspirational posts prompted them to like a status update. Surprisingly, only 23% said they like a post that has a baby, pet or selfie in it. I found this interesting because it contradicts what many people have said for years. Humor was another factor in what someone liked.

Once you comment on a post on Facebook, you get notifications every time someone responds to that post. In our survey, we asked: "Do you continue to read the thread, or do you stop the notifications?" Interestingly there was a split in whether or not people continued to follow the thread. More than 40% said they enjoyed reading, while nearly 40% said they leave the conversation once they post. Many people said it depended on what the post was about.

One of the responders said, "It depends on how engaged I am. For example, congratulations posts never require additional reading. Advice seeking posts often make for good follow up reads to see what others have suggested."

There was a three-way tie when it came to what type of post interested most people. Seventy percent said a well-written post, an informative post, and a humorous post interested them. Many people said that personal posts interest them while others said a post that they don't agree with was one that interested them.

Sixty-eight percent said they would comment on a post to encourage or congratulate someone. Many said they would comment on a post if they disagreed with it and want their point to be heard. After supporting their friends with a like, 61% said they would comment to make a witty comment or joke on a post.

And 85% said they read a posted blog before liking it on Facebook.

How about tagging? Nearly 65% said they don't like to be tagged, especially in a post that has nothing to do with them.

When reading the newsfeed on Facebook, how does it make you feel? There's been much talk about the subject, and many say that Facebook tends to make people sad because of the depressing posts that people have on their status updates.

When asked why posts make them feel a particular way, there was a range of answers including:

"I have too many friends at this point. They've gathered over the years, and I don't know about 80% of the people I'm friends with. So, my newsfeed is just full of things I don't care about."

"I look at Facebook when I'm bored."

"Sometimes I see some stupid news articles, or sometimes I see something a friend has achieved, one makes me feel bad, the other is a nice thing to see."

"I read my feed with a grain of salt. It's a bizarre representation of people's actual lives."

"Too many of my friends post links and memes instead of posting about their lives."

"I've unfollowed updates from almost everyone since it's either boring or stupid. So basically, all I see are updates from 5-6 friends, bands, or sports news sites."

If someone posts things that are annoying or that prompt disagreement, nearly 50% said they would unfollow the person.

One of the respondents said, "I start by debating or correcting factual errors in specific posts; if the person persists in posting the same misleading or inaccurate information despite links and other evidence to the contrary, I will unsubscribe to further activity on the thread. If a person keeps posting memes and other worthless content, I hide these. If a person engages in ad hominem attacks or threats, I block that person."

So, what does this all mean?

People want to see posts that are personal and meaningful. They generally don't want to hear about things that are irrelevant to them. Facebook is a place to disseminate information, whether personal, news-related, or opinion-based. People want to be helpful and congratulate their friends and provide relevant feedback to questions and items of interest. Above all, Facebook is very personalized to the user, giving each person control over their experiences by what they comment on, whom they block and the things they like.

✎ My Observation…

Of all the social media sites I am on, I like the interaction and the conversation starters from Facebook best. It's been a great place to conduct business by solidifying contacts. I always seem to get a dialogue going with someone I value. Facebook has helped increase visitors to my blog. I've used Facebook since 2007 and have seen substantial growth in terms of the number of people who follow me. This has resulted in a significant increase in business. All of my clients are on Facebook and tend to direct message me on Messenger throughout the day with questions. I love that it's instantaneous, but I don't like that I can't turn it off. I have it on all day and all night in case someone wants to send me an urgent message. The days of working 9 a.m. to 5 p.m. are long over.

Many people ask me if they should have a personal page and a business page. I tell them they should have both. The business page will not get much in terms of engagement, unless you boost the post. However, it's important to have a business presence on Facebook. I find that business for my firm is developed on my personal page. I think it makes sense. People want to connect with other people. They don't see a business page as relatable. The business page is important to offer information about the business and that's it. On your personal page, you can direct message people and build lasting relationships that may lead to business development.

If Facebook makes sense for you in targeting your buyer persona, then remember to add it to your integrated marketing plan.

INSTA YOU, INSTA ME, INSTAGRAM

"The beauty of pictures and a story, in a way that emphasizes imagery first - it's the cat's pajamas." Meredith Atwood, "Swim Bike Mom" Blog, Author of **The Year of No Nonsense**, Boston, MA

On January 4, 2019, the most-liked post on Instagram was a photograph of a brown egg,[45] with nearly 54 million likes. This was posted by @world_record_egg and beat Kylie Jenner's post announcing the birth of her daughter, Stormi, which prompted 18 million likes, according to CBS. In response to the egg post, Kylie tried to sizzle an egg on the ground but only got 4 million likes.

Instagram is one of the leading social networking sites, with more than 2 billion active users. According to Instagram,[46] more than 200 million businesses are using its platform, and that number seems to grow exponentially every year.

Instagram wants to keep people on the site for as long as possible and will reward users for this engagement by helping them with their SEO on the site.

⚡ How to Use Instagram

There are currently four ways to use Instagram – a static post, a story, Reels or Live.

⚡ A Static Post

A static post is a photo. According to Omnicore Agency, there are more than 50 billion photos shared on Instagram.[47] Photos could be of anything that depicts and represents your brand.

Some ideas include:

- Staff or volunteers in action
- Happy customers
- Products in use
- Food
- Statistics

Post regularly, but don't over-post or you will lose followers. Also, comment on other photos to build engagement. I recommend that you post one time per day but, if you consistently post two to three times a week, that would work as well. The more times you post in a week (not a day) the higher your position in the algorithm. If you post once in a while, you will move down in the algorithm and no one will see your posts.

◔ Instagram Story

You can make a story just about anything. Make sure there is a beginning, middle, and end. Many people only post one short 15-second video although some people post a video, a photograph, another video, and more within the story. Each component makes up part of a story. On the photos or video, you can also add comments, emojis, a time and location tag, and you can also post a date to your stories. You can even ask questions to your community. You may want to do this for your brand because it better connects you with your community in a fun and engaging way and can help determine what your community might like or dislike. You may consider polling on your stories to see what your consumers want. Many fashion brands, for example, will do this to poll their consumers with various styles, fabrics and more to see what they should consider for the following season.

The beauty of stories is that it appears on the top of your followers' feed for only 24 hours, making it immediate. If you don't see the story, you will miss out!

If your story has importance or you want to save the entire story, you can add it to your profile by highlighting and preserving it.

◔ Instagram Reels

Instagram Reels is a feature within the Instagram app that allows users to create and share short, engaging videos. Inspired by the popularity of TikTok, Reels provides a platform for Instagram users to record 15 to 90-second video clips set to music or other audio and share them on their feed, Explore tab, or the new Reels tab on a user's profile. Users can enhance their videos with creative tools like filters, effects, and speed controls. Since its launch in August 2020, Instagram Reels has emerged as a significant player in the short-form video content space, offering a new way for creators and businesses to engage and entertain their audience.

☝ Instagram Live

Instagram Live is a feature within the Instagram app that allows users to broadcast videos to their followers in real time. Part of Instagram's Stories, Live videos give you an opportunity to connect with your audience in an immediate, unscripted manner. Users can comment on, like, or share live videos, creating interactive and engaging conversations. Once a live video has ended, it can be saved to Instagram or deleted, disappearing from the app. Whether it's for Q&A sessions, product launches, tutorials, or just casual check-ins, Instagram Live offers a unique platform for real-time engagement.

☝ Hashtags

Hashtags help you get noticed. Search some relevant hashtags first on Instagram by clicking the magnifying glass and typing in your search criteria. You would be amazed at how many hashtags there are. Make sure to use one that has ample followers so that your message gets seen.

At the printing of this publication, according to Wix Blog,[48] the most popular hashtags are: #beautiful, #cute, #instagood,

#instamood, #like4like, #love, #me, #picoftheday, #photooftheday, and #tbt.

It's essential to develop a list of your hashtags and then run a search and see if there are followers and enough to attract more people to your page.

I developed a list of hashtags that I rotate. Depending on which account I post a photo to, I change the hashtags. To do this most efficiently, I post the hashtags in a note on my iPhone. Then, I copy and paste it into the Instagram comment box.

Some people position their hashtags so that they appear below their post by adding a period, then returning, and adding a period until about ten periods appear on the post.

Here's an example from a recent post:

"It felt good to soak my feet in the cold fountain after a day of golf! Triathlon training has definitely helped my #golf game.

.

.

.

.

.

.

#golf #playinggolf #merrickgolfcourse #callowaygolf #titlist #titlistgolf #callowayballs #triathlete #triathlon

Notice how I included "periods" to drop down the copy to the hashtag? Some people do this so that the hashtags appear in the original post but when pushing the Instagram photo out to Facebook and X, the hashtags don't appear.

You can also include hashtags by putting them in the comment box under your post. I tend to use this method for my Instagram posts because it's easier to do and it gets the same results.

You can post up to 30 hashtags per post.

✍ Posting Strategies

To get the most of your Instagram posts, consider the following. Do your photos reflect who you are? Are you posting a high-quality photo? Are they blurry? What's the focus of the photo?

According to the *Huffington Post*,[49] here are steps you should take:

- Make a plan. What is your feed about and what direction should you take with it?
- Don't get hung up on how many likes you get from a post.
- When taking a photo, try to use natural lighting. Make sure the sun is behind you. Otherwise the picture may come out much darker than you would like.
- Put up exciting photos with compelling captions.
- Seek out a specific place to photograph yourself.

When taking photographs, here are a few essential things to consider:

- Does the photo tell a story?
- Try different angles – get down, stand up on a chair, do something different so that there's more interest in the photo.
- Pay attention to the background. (At my first triathlon, at the finish line, I had someone take a photo of me. I didn't notice that there were porta-potties in the background. Not the picture I would have wanted!)
- Determine where the sun is. If you shoot into the sun, your photo will be dark and take on a different flavor than you may have wanted.
- Look for interesting places to shoot. An exciting photo will go a long way.

☼ Free Photography Sites

I wouldn't suggest posting stock photos on Instagram unless you genuinely have no other choice. If that's the case, check out these free photography sites:

- Pixaby.com.
- Unsplash.com.
- Pexels.com.

If you use a "free" image be sure to read the fine print. If these photo sites ask you to credit the photographer, do it. Don't grab a photo from Google without permission. You will pay dearly for it. A violation of the terms of use can subject you to a copyright claim.

☼ Written Content for the Post

The more I research and evaluate text that is written for Instagram, the more I realize you need to tell a story. If you're doing this for your business, tie it into your organization without being salesy or people will lose interest. Your buyers want to get to know you – the real you – before they purchase your product or service. People also want to read a story. Be a storyteller and engage your community.

You may even want to repurpose content that is posted by your brand ambassador to diversify your content and add credibility.

♨ Demographics of Instagram Users

With more than 1.3 billion images shared every day, Instagram is the third most popular social site, according to Hootsuite.[50] Here are some specifics:

- There are more than 2+ billion active monthly users.
- 50% females and 50% male.
- 82% are college educated.
- Majority of the users are between 18 and 29.

♨ My Observation...

I love Instagram. I find there is a lot of engagement there, and I get to have an inside peek into my community. Concurrently, my community gets an inside look into my life. It's an excellent tool for personal branding, and with the right photos and content, you can attract the proper attention for your brand. Remember, the demographics for Instagram are different from Facebook. It's a little younger so, make sure your posts appeal to them.

Tip: You will be solicited by companies trying to sell you followers. Be wary and don't do it. By purchasing followers, you are only hurting yourself in the long run. Most of the followers that you will be buying are not real people.

Will Instagram attract the right audience for you? If so, put it in your integrated marketing plan.

DO YOU REALLY NEED TO BE ON LINKEDIN?

"I think of LinkedIn as the online version of networking, not the online version of a cold call. If you meet someone in person you wouldn't try to sell them immediately – at least I hope you wouldn't. You need to grow the relationship, learn about the other person, offer value first. Engaging with other people in your target market helps cut through the noise. Engage with content that others share! People don't often think about this as a strategy, but it's a good one." Beth Granger, Owner, Beth Granger Consulting & LinkedIn Coach, Long Island, NY

Evolved since its conception, LinkedIn is one of the most popular business sites with use for business purposes only. You can see a stream of information from your community. You can connect and network with others by participating in polls, joining groups, and sharing expertise.

Through the years, LinkedIn has become very similar to Facebook in its look and accessibility.

The LinkedIn homepage provides a list of network updates, broadcasting what business contacts are doing and with whom they are connecting.

The homepage provides a constructive newsfeed that is based on its members' interests. If you are interested in marketing, for example, you will find that LinkedIn offers all of the RSS feeds on marketing topics for your reading pleasure.

Also, the homepage offers other valuable information, including events in your area of expertise as well as job opportunities. It also provides a chance to ask and answer industry-related questions.

The more robust your profile, the more likely others will be drawn to learn about you. List all of your work experience and your current position, so that former colleagues and clients can easily find you. On the homepage, you can assess if your profile is working by viewing how many page hits it received.

There are groups that you can join and various companies that you can search. Like Facebook, LinkedIn has multiple applications that enables members to promote their work and build a following. If a member decides to start a group, the member will be showcased as a thought-leader. However, even if you don't create a group, consider joining one to meet new people and foster new relationships.

Perhaps one of the best features of LinkedIn is its application to help others, showcase expertise, and receive valuable business advice. Often, high-level dialogues about business ensue.

And there is the valuable potential to reach out to people with whom you might have otherwise lost touch. Recently three old friends contacted me on LinkedIn – one now lives in Chicago, another in Minnesota and the third in Denver. I hadn't seen them in nearly 20 years. It was exciting to hear from them, and by reconnecting, I broadened my business pool and increased my community outreach. Without LinkedIn, I don't think I would be in contact with them.

☝ Personalizing Your Profile

The profile on this site is similar to that of a resume. Personalize the profile by uploading a photo of yourself. Then, include information such as current job position, past job positions, and education. The more information you provide, the more easily clients and colleagues – past and present – will find you.

☝ Making Connections

When you make a connection on LinkedIn, you will be connected with that person in the 1st degree. Your contacts have their own contacts. Their contacts to you are called 2nd degree. The 3rd degree is contacts' contacts' contacts. You can ultimately meet anyone in the 2nd or 3rd degree with an introduction from one of your connections. This level of introduction serves as both an endorsement for you and an opportunity to connect with someone you want to meet.

☝ Recommendations

Contact previous or even current employers or business colleagues on LinkedIn to request a recommendation of your work for your profile. This is useful when building your professional reputation and looking for potential jobs or clients. Through the recommendations tab, keep track of recommendation requests, recommendations sent, and ones received.

○ Website

Post URLs for your company's websites, blogs, and so on for contacts to view.

○ About

Create a summary of your company and work experience, as well as your specialty areas. This area is very similar to a resume and mission statement. Be as specific as possible.

○ Article Writing

On LinkedIn, you have an opportunity to share your thoughts and views on any subject with your community. This is a perfect place to position yourself as a thought-leader.

○ Contacts

After creating a profile, find/invite contacts using LinkedIn's finder. There are six ways to add contacts:

- Upload your address book from your email account, and LinkedIn will find those who are on the site.

- Input your old classmates' names, and LinkedIn will search its database for matches.
- Post the URL in your email signature. This will help contacts from other sites find you. Also include the link on other social networking sites like Facebook and X.
- Use the People Tab at the top of the homepage to search for specific contacts and request to connect.
- Get in touch with past colleagues through the connections tab and by placing information about previous jobs on the profile.
- Invite contacts to your network through the add connections tab by entering their first and last name and email.

☝ Videos

Videos have become a popular tool on LinkedIn. You can use them to introduce your product or service to the LinkedIn community. Or, you can use LinkedIn live to show a seminar in which you are participating. This helps to share your expertise on your brand.

☝ Groups

LinkedIn has an abundance of groups to join to help you increase your number of contacts. Add groups to your profile that are of interest and can better serve you or your company. To form a group, click on the "create a group" tab and follow the step-by-step instructions.

☼ InMail

Send and receive messages from contacts through LinkedIn's email system, called InMail. Click on the inbox tab and then compose the message. This method allows contact with other members while keeping messages private. You can also chat with someone in real time. You can only InMail those connections in your community. However, if you want to send an InMail to someone not in your community, you can by purchasing the premium version of LinkedIn. This enables you to connect with someone you may not otherwise connect to and is a powerful part of LinkedIn. For example, if you are a financial advisor and you are looking to target someone at a large law firm you recognize, with the premium version, you can send that person an InMail stating why you want to connect with them.

☼ Jobs

Search for available jobs posted by others by clicking on the jobs tab. Enter the kind of job and location sought, and LinkedIn then searches the database for matches. In addition, LinkedIn is a great way to connect with recruiters. So, make sure your profile is up-to-date with your latest job description.

☼ Companies

Use this link to browse industries and companies on LinkedIn, which lists them according to your profile entries. This feature provides another way to make connections on the site. For example, you may find people you know listed in the breakdown. Alternatively, you may find contact information for those you would like to meet at other companies.

♨ Business Page

It's good to have a business page for branding. But, in terms of connecting with your target market, create a personal profile so that you can share information as well on the personal page and connect to your audience on a one-on-one basis. On the business page, share information about what's happening in your organization. Did you have a new hire? Do you have a new product offering? Make sure this is up-to-date and that you post at least once or twice a week.

♨ LinkedIn Premium

While LinkedIn is a free social networking site, it does provide an option to upgrade to a paid account. Those who pay for the site gain access to additional networking tools and can deliver messages to people who have secure privacy settings. In addition, the paid-for version lets you see who has looked at your profile. This enables you to try to pitch those who have viewed your profile because they already show an interest in you and your company.

Another feature is LinkedIn Learning, which enables you to access thousands of business, tech and design courses. LinkedIn Learning uses content from Lynda.com, a company they acquired. As a premium customer, you will get a "daily bite" on your feed.

Case Studies

Case studies are abundant on LinkedIn. Here are a couple of examples of how major companies increased their ROI:

Docusign[51] is a company that has become well-known for their eSignatures on various documents. The firm partnered with LinkedIn by sponsoring the platform's InMail in bulk by geo-locations. InMail, as discussed above, is a powerful tool because Docusign's message went directly to the inbox of their target audience. As a result, the company's sales rose 45%.

Postcard Mania,[52] a Florida-based marketing company, conducted a campaign on LinkedIn. Postcard Mania posted "8 Ways to Grow Your Local Business for FREE!" This post included a landing page where potential customers could input their emails and other important information. As a result, they collected 600 emails and generated $72,000 in income. They also provided concrete tips and strategies to niche markets with URL's linking to landing pages. Postcard Mania also had their CEO's post messages in groups offering valuable marketing tactics. This further generated more revenue for the company and they continue to use LinkedIn as one of their main sources for leads and referrals.

Demographics of LinkedIn Users

According to Omnicore Agency,[53] LinkedIn, which started in 2003, has more than 900 million users.

- There are more than 49 million weekly active users. However, 199+ million are from the United States.

- 57% are male.
- 87 million millennials.
- Sixty-one million are senior-level influencers.
- Sixty-five million are actual decision-makers.

⤻ My Observation...

I find LinkedIn useful for business and, through the years, have generated business through the site. However, I find that most of the people on LinkedIn are also looking for business. It becomes a lot of clutter and stuffed inboxes. As a result, it is probably my least favorite site. I would much prefer getting to know someone on a personal level before doing business with them, and Facebook lets me do just that. I find that most people have a LinkedIn profile, but not all people are active on LinkedIn. The direct messages are a little invasive, and most of the comments made to me are irrelevant.

Tip: Make sure your network is solid. Don't just accept random people. This way, you will have a better chance of success on the site. LinkedIn Learning also makes the site more valuable because being successful in business means that you have to consistently learn.

Does LinkedIn make sense for your brand? If so, make sure to add to your integrated marketing plan under tactics!

WHO

WHO KNOCKED ON THE NEXTDOOR?

"I like Nextdoor because you can connect with neighbors and get feedback on things that are going on in the area. This hyper-local site enables you to connect with your neighbors. It is used to keep up with community news, talk with neighbors, find out about job opportunities, and ask for recommendations." Carla Schultheis, Neighbor, Long Island, NY

Nextdoor is an excellent place for small businesses to get referrals and traction. When you log in, you are assigned an area in which you live. For example, my neighborhood is called the Margaret Blvd Group. Here, I see my neighbors asking for recommendations or thoughts about a particular vendor. I've used it to get a cleaning service for my home and I also asked for a recommendation for a gardener.

Other people have asked for recommendations on solar companies, pizzerias, and other random topics. The bottom line is, you can get business from this site if you have ambassadors who have used your services.

In addition to viewing the feed with various questions and topics from neighbors, you can also create groups. Most recently, I created a running group and looked forward to meeting runners from around the neighborhood.

anthony Lombardo, North Bellmore Newbridge   F   1

ELECTRICIAN FOR HIRE

Hey guys my name is Anthony If anyone is looking for an electrician with 15+ yrs of experience. I do all kinds of residential / commercial work including :

renovations and or new construction...
-indoor and outdoor lighting
-tv's Hung and wires tucked and hidden
-add or relocate outlets
-Fans installs
-low voltage
-security cameras
-ring doorbells / floodlight cameras
-landscape lighting
-panel upgrades

You name it I can do it and I'm very fair priced ... call , text or email if you need help with anything

Alombardo120@gmail.com
516-578-0931

19 hr ago · 23 neighborhoods in General

Thank   Reply ∨

Nextdoor works very similarly to other social networking sites. It is user-friendly and you can get started immediately. When you scroll through the page, you will see either vendors trying to sell their products or services, as seen above with Anthony, the electrician.

In the "neighborhood section" on the righthand side, you will see a list of different subheads that are clickable. If you click on the "business" section, you will be able to see recommended businesses from your neighbors. There is a "For Sale" section, which is similar to Facebook's Marketplace or Craigslist, where you can sell anything from a couch to a drum set.

In addition to that, you can post local events, like a grand opening or a kickoff event for a new group. There's a lost and found section, crime and safety section and even a section for "local deals," where you might offer a discount for your services to neighbors.

Be careful of how you position yourself. The point with this site is to try to create lasting relationships with neighbors.

☝ Demographics

Unfortunately, there are no substantiated demographics at the printing of this publication. However, from looking at the site, it seems as if most of the people in my area are between 35 and 65. They seem to be established homeowners.

☝ My Observation...

If you own a local business, you can introduce yourself on Nextdoor. You can also recruit some of your "ambassadors" to talk about your restaurant, your service, or your product on Nextdoor. These reviews will help increase visibility and awareness and help your business grow. Hyperlocal sites are great for business networking because customers are in your immediate area.

If you have a business that is neighborhood centric or could be, this may be a great site for you. Make sure to put Nextdoor on your integrated marketing plan under tactics.

WHAT DO YOU PIN ON PINTEREST?

"What I love the most about Pinterest is everything is in one place and I can pin from so many other blogs and sites. I have everything saved under categories with just a click. It's the best site. I use it all the time." Kathy Cittadino Munsch, Former Vice President, American Heart Association, Long Island, NY

What is Pinterest?

Did you ever have a bulletin board in your home or office? Well, if you did, think of Pinterest as such. Pinterest is a series of virtual bulletin boards that hold pins. For example, a bride-to-be may use Pinterest to organize her wedding. On one board, she might pin wedding dresses that she is interested in trying on. On another board, she may pin various venues in which to hold her wedding.

♨ Where to Start

Start by creating a profile and creating pins. Alternatively, scan through the site and see what appeals to you, re-pinning it to your board. Sometimes, I find podcasts on Pinterest that I want to listen to, and I save them to a private board that only I have access to, which enables me to go back and listen when I can. You can have as many public boards as you want. You can also create private or secret boards that only you can see.

♨ Video on Pinterest

Now you can create a video, similar to Instagram or Facebook. You can pin this video on one of your boards to help increase engagement.

♨ Claiming Accounts

You can link your Etsy account, your Instagram account, and even your YouTube account to Pinterest. This will enable you to direct traffic to your other accounts as you build your brand. The platform also enables you to connect the site to other apps like Poshmark. This is an interesting feature if you own a craft or clothing business.

♨ Notifications

Notifications allow you to see what your friends in your community are doing – whether they are creating new boards, pinning something new and other activities. Notifications also provide the opportunity to direct message someone as you would on Facebook or any of the other social sites.

♨ How Can Your Business Benefit?

Pinterest is a great site for any visual type business. If you own jewelry store, a restaurant, or if you make crafts sold on Etsy, this site is for you. But, Pinterest is also for corporations. Here, consumers can get an inside look at who you are and what you do. Even journalists, bloggers, or podcasters can benefit because you can promote your media outlet on Pinterest by creating various boards. Non-profit organizations or cause marketing can also benefit from Pinterest by generating boards that show what you are doing. Some CEO's use Pinterest as a platform to give their community an inside look at what the CEO likes and how the CEO gives back to the community. As you are well aware, commonalities are ice breakers that can help you lead to doing business.

♨ Noteworthy Pinterest Campaign

Although this isn't a new campaign, I still love it. Honda[54] asked its community to take a break from Pinterest for 24 hours. The automaker selected five of the top pinners to participate in this break and offered them $500 each to do whatever they wanted, as long as they stayed off Pinterest. As a result, more than 4.6 million people were exposed on Pinterest to Honda and the campaign. When the campaign finished, there were 5,000 re-pins, nearly 2,000 likes and it only cost the brand $2,500. Sounds like good ROI to me!

When Barak Obama was running for president in 2009, he had a great Pinterest page. His boards focused on food from the campaign trail, dogs of the White House, photos of his family, and more. You got to take a personal look at the man he is, and you felt a connection. In this way, Pinterest played a big part in his campaign.

Hillary Clinton, on the other hand, tried to follow President Obama's footsteps by creating a Pinterest page similar to his. However, she fell short by not being forthcoming about her life and seeming reserved. This came through on the social boards she posted.

♂ Demographics of Pinterest Users

According to Omnicore Agency,[55] there are more than 450 million active Pinterest users.

- 80% of the pinners live outside the US.
- 46% of US woman adults use Pinterest.

♂ My Observation...

Any business can benefit from Pinterest. Businesses that are visual tend to do very well on this site. Large corporation can benefit too by showing their products, services and community outreach efforts. It's important to show who you are, especially if you are in the political arena or a CEO of a service company. Many people are drawn to the visual aspects of this site and it will help enable others to feel connected with you.

The integration with Esty, makes selling easy. This site would work great for jewelry designers, chefs and pastry chefs, real estate brokers, party planners, or anyone in the creative/ visual space.

If you feel this site fits into your integrated marketing plan, include it in the tactics section.

WHAT

WHAT QUESTIONS DO YOU HAVE FOR QUORA?

"I find that Quora can be beneficial when it comes to developing storylines, angles, or engaging and interacting with other people's opinions." Jacqueline Gruber, Technology PR, Highwire PR, NYC

If you want to position yourself as a thought-leader, then Quora is an ideal site for you.

Quora is a question-and-answer site that requires people to use their real names. They discourage low-quality answers. This is an excellent source for anyone willing to spend time answering questions in areas where they have expertise.

Users ask questions about anything and everything. So that you don't miss an opportunity to share your knowledge, make sure to sign up for topics that interest you.

Customize your interests on the homepage. For example, I love running, so that is one of my categories. I'm also in a wearable tech group and get posed interesting questions like, "Why did Google stop production on Google Glass for consumers?"

The newest feature is "Spaces." This enables people to curate content and form communities around shared interests. This allows users to work together on shared content. You can also use the space to organize your content, or to talk about a specific topic.

With Spaces, you can follow any of the dozens of groups or create your own group.

And on Quora you can define what topics you want people to ask you. This sets the site apart from other social networking sites.

⚘ Demographics

Unfortunately, Quora doesn't track the demographics of the site.

⚘ My Observation...

Quora is great for professionals looking to get in front of an audience that is interested in a particular subject.

If you want to become a thought-leader in a particular field, then include Quora in your integrated marketing plan.

DID YOU READ IT ON REDDIT?

"Working in the public sector means every audience is one of our target audiences. From commuters to residents, other government entities to businesses, we have messages to convey that need to be relevant, timely, useful and on the platform of choice. For talking to our residents, we love Nextdoor and Reddit. They both drive great engagement." Shannah Hayley, FSMPS, CPSM, Director of Communications & Community Outreach, City of Plano, TX

Reddit is an engaging social media site because it is all crowd-generated content. Most of the time, you won't know who you are talking to on this site. With 330 million[56] unique active users, that's a lot of people!

How Does It Work?

Once you create an account, you can customize your homepage with topics that interest you. On my homepage, I have topics that include social media marketing, running, and triathlon.

On the left-hand side, you will see arrows pointing up or down with a number. This is the number of "upvotes and/or downvotes" a post gets. You can also comment on the thread.

Every group has a subgroup, and each has several threads. You can create your subgroup or participate in an existing one. There are 1.2 million subreddit groups, so look for those in your category of expertise.

In the subgroup, you can listen to what your potential consumers are talking about. This can help you tailor messages to this community.

The right-hand side features several boxes that include the top-trending topics and the top-trending communities. You can join any of these, or just read the posts.

If you read a post and like it, you can upvote it. If you don't like it, you can downvote it. The more you get downvoted, the more likely it is that you will not be able to post on Reddit. The more upvotes you get, the more likely you will get "Karma," and will be able to continue to post on the site.

How Can Businesses Use Reddit?

Here are seven ways for businesses to make the most of Reddit.

1) Engage with customers and find out what interests them.
2) Create a subreddit group and use that for customer service.
3) Find a community through subreddit groups.
4) Use the subreddit group to post your calendar or event schedule.
5) Feature an influencer or celebrity through a Q & A.

6) Assess market trends.

7) Hold a contest.

Business can also advertise on Reddit in specific subgroups. For example, if your target market is information technology, then you can advertise specifically in that group with a customized message to direct people to either a landing page or your website for more information.

Demographics of Reddit Users

According to *TechJunkie*[57] Reddit was founded in 2005 by two 22-year-olds from the University of Virginia. The stats reveal that:

· There are 330 million active users.
· The majority are between 18 and 29.
· 49% are male and 51% are female.
· The majority have some college education.

My Observation...

Reddit is a great site to monitor and to see trends. You can get a ton of feedback on the site, and the content isn't sugar-coated. It's raw, honest and it works.

Consider joining a Reddit subgroup and getting involved. You may even create one in your area of expertise. This will enable you to moderate the content and see what interests others. Then you can use the information you gather to help market your business.

If Reddit is in your appropriate target market, then consider including it in your integrated marketing plan.

SNAP ON SNAPCHAT

"*Snapchat is a great app to use when wanting to communicate with friends and family about fun adventures. I often use Snapchat as a way to let people in my life know about things that I am doing without posting it on Facebook for everyone to see. My closest friends are the ones that I have on Snapchat versus having my Facebook account where there are hundreds of people that can see what I am doing. I thoroughly enjoy the filters that Snapchat creates and like creating my own to document various activities and adventures.*" Erin Seader, Pediatric Occupational Therapy Assistant, Eaton, CO

Many people ask me if Snapchat is going to fade away like so many of the other social networking sites that were popular in the past, including Plaxo, Friendfeed, and Foursquare. However, according to Statista, Snapchat will continue to grow into 2030.

Today, there are more than 375 million unique Snapchat users.[58] In the United States and Canada, more than 101 million are active users. Ninety percent of the Snapchat users are between 13 and 24 years old.

○ How Does It Work?

First, create a profile. Snapchat allows you to send personal "snaps" to your friends or your connections through the chat feature. It is also linked with Bitmoji, which allows you to create an avatar or "Bitmoji," a caricature of you. You use this as your profile icon.

When you click on the "discover" icon, you can see what your friends are sharing. You can also see what businesses are sharing. There is the ability to sponsor, or boost, a story so that it gets more exposure with an audience. If you are targeting a group, make sure your story appeals to that audience.

○ What Can Small Businesses Do With Snapchat?

Here are several strategies businesses can use on Snapchat to engage their community.

- Post stories on Snapchat. Stories are a series of videos or photographs strung together to create something meaningful for your community. Remember that you are marketing to Gen Z'ers. What would attract their interest and attention?
- Upload stories every day.
- Engage and talk with other people on Snapchat.
- Try Snapchat filters and lenses to enhance your story.

- Invite a social media influencer on Snapchat to take over your account for an hour, a day, or even a month. You will have to pay them for this service.
- Ask your community to submit photos or videos of themselves using your product or service, and re-post on the page.
- Offer discounts, promos, or both, to your community.
- Promote events.
- Create geo-filters.

♂ Case Study

BMW X2[59] wanted to attract millennials and GenZ'ers. The company went to Snapchat to conduct a worldwide ad campaign and engage with its potential community. They created a "world lens," and consumers had to swipe up on the ad to unlock the lens. A world lens is a 3D image that is created by the app and when someone takes a photo of something within the app, the 3D image appears.

By opening the lens, with augmented reality, Snapchatters turned into gold, which was essentially a gold filter. The community loved the campaign, and as a result, BMW had 40 million impressions on the face lens, and one in four people shared or saved the X2 lens.

♂ Demographics of Snapchat Users:

- There are 375 million active users on Snapchat.
- The majority of users are under 34 years old.
- 61% are female and 38% are male.
- Most of the users have some college.

☝ My Observation…

If you have a business where millennials and specifically GenZ'ers are your audience, then consider using Snapchat. There are lots of creative things you can do to attract this community. Augmented reality is already in place and can be used to make awareness of a brand in a fun and unique way.

If Snapchat users are your buyer persona, then remember to include in your integrated marketing plan.

TIKTOK TOE

"*I began posting to Musical.ly (now TikTok) early on, after meeting some of its early stars at the Shorty Awards, and discovering that the platform enjoyed both a rapidly growing user base and unusually high engagement metrics and levels of user retention. While I knew from the start that TikTok's userbase was significantly younger than my general target audience, and that I would need to adopt my messaging on the platform for its demographics, I also knew that time flies, and that, in just a few years, many "musers" would begin exploring professions and entering the workforce. As such, while TikTok has never been my primary mechanism for communicating with my audience, I do use it in order to reach people who I otherwise would not reach, and who, eventually, will become part of my primary target audience.*" Joseph Steinberg, Columnist and Advisor to Cybersecurity and Emerging Technology Companies, NYC

Do you remember the social site, Vine, a video platform that allowed users to create a 10-second video and worked in conjunction with X? TikTok[60] is similar, except TikTok is an independent site.

Previously owned by Musica.ly, TikTok is a video sharing social site. Many people use it to lip-sync, dance, or both, to their favorite song. Others use it to brand their image, product or service in a unique way.

The format features a 15 or 60 second video, with a continuous loop, on anything and everything. You can also upload photos and create a collage with music in the background.

It works similar to other social networking sites. Users generate hashtags and content that appear within the video. You can also comment on a video and, even appear within it. There are less hashtags used on TikTok and most of the hashtags are #fyp or #foryourpage.

Scrolling through the TikTok feed, you get a sense of the types of videos that seem to go viral and generate engagement. The funnier the video is, the more engagement it gets.

The site is clever, uplifting, and simply hilarious. On TikTok, I watched a woman in a suit drinking beer on her way to work. She lip-syncs, "You're damn right I'm having a beer, have you been to my f-ing job?" (@charitybird).

☝ Who Uses TikTok?

Originally conceived in China, TikTok has its biggest base there, followed by India. In the United States, there have been more than 220 million downloads. The site is available worldwide.

The largest user group is people between 16 and 24. However, the site is also popular with millennials, Gen Y and Baby Boomers.

☼ What Can You Do With TikTok to Help Your Brand?

You can record a video directly on TikTok, add sound, create effects, play around with the speed (by either using slow-motion or by speeding up the video) and you can add filters. The music library is robust and works with Apple Music.

In addition, you can share a video you love with your community from Snapchat, Instagram, Instagram Stories, Facebook, Messenger, Text, X, WhatsApp, etc. You can comment on others' posts and give them a heart if you like what they are doing.

There are duets, where you can take someone's video and add yourself to it to form a new post for your page. TikTok's "react" is another interesting feature. Here, you can react to another person's video by placing your reaction within the video to form a new video. (If your account is private, you can't add a reaction.)

☼ Brands Using TikTok

Chipotle[61] uses TikTok to build awareness for its Mexican fast food chain. The company has created interesting videos making guacamole and posting photos of its food to music. If you search for Chipotle you will see a handful of user-generated videos about the brand, helping to build awareness about the chain.

Through the app, the NBA highlights basketball games and motivational quotes from players. The association does this to show the personal side of the brand.

Believe it or not the Washington Post and the San Diego Zoo have TikTok accounts and show behind-the-scenes stories that are engaging, light and fun.

Interestingly, the algorithm works as soon as you start flipping through the videos. If you stop and look at one of the same type of videos, when you come back, you will continue to see what you like to look at. For example, I stopped and watched a few of the dog videos set to music. Now, every time I open the app, I see dog videos.

👍 Tips on Using TikTok

Here are some helpful tips for using TikTok for your brand:

- Use creativity to show another dimension to your company. This allows your community to see the "fun" side of you and enables them to connect with you.
- Experiment with different options. "If you think something might be interesting or funny, try it and see if it gets any likes, comments, or shares," according to Hubspot.
- Try to engage as much as possible. Jimmy Fallon[62] tested his audience to participate in a "tumble weed" challenge, asking members of his community to go on TikTok and create a video rolling on the ground like tumble weed. This challenge got 28.4 million views, with thousands of interesting videos.

I just started to post on TikTok and have seen a tremendous amount of engagement and views, which I find intriguing. It's incredible the growth of this site.

☝ Demographics

The parent company of TikTok doesn't like to share information about the demographics but, we know the following:

- The majority of TikTok users are GenZer's (Ages 16 – 24)
- The majority are female.

☝ My Observation...

If your brand targets Gen Z'ers, then a presence on TikTok is a must, and this should be included in your integrated marketing plan. I think the site will continue to grow, and as it does, it may get bought out by some of the major players. But, in the meantime, create a strategy for your brand that would be fun, exciting and different. Then, share on TikTok, and see what happens.

DID YOU TUMBLE ON TUMBLR?

"What I love about Tumblr is that it gives me a place to become a better thinker. Whether I'm taking in the words and works of others or are putting out my own content, I'm learning, laughing, and slowly becoming a more aware person." Jenna Pace, Account Clerk Special Education Department, NYC

When searching for Tumblr, don't make the same mistake I made and type in Tumbler.com, because if you do, you will end up on Travis Tumbler's site, which sells tumbling cups. You will shake your head and walk away.

Tumblr, which is a play on the word, tumblelog, is a variation of a blog, except instead of entries, users make short posts or microblogs as if on X. However, this is more of a blog site than X. It is ideal for someone who wants to be on a social networking site or wants to have a blog, but does not have time to update or make new entries. As with other social media platforms, you will want the site to showcase your brand.

♻ Personalizing Your Profile

Customize a Tumblr page as if you were customizing a blog. Customize tumblelogs with the following:

♻ Information

Give the tumblelog a title, add data, and upload a portrait.

♻ Theme

Choose the theme from a list of different customized themes already created or if you are comfortable hand-coding, work with HTML to create your own theme.

♻ Appearance

Modify the appearance of your tumblelog by selecting the color of the page. Choose the default color or change the colors on a page for each of the following items:

- Background
- Text
- Link
- Header
- Date Text
- Image Border
- Image Background
- Previous/Next Tab
- Footer Border

♻ Advanced Tailoring

Tailor your site by changing time zones, advertising on the tumblelog, and adding custom cascading style sheets (CSS), which adds style to web pages or blogs. The Tumblr dashboard is your profile and is very easy to navigate.

♻ Dashboard Features

This dashboard offers various controls for your account. Here is a run-down.

- **Show All Posts**: Select this feature to see who is following you, who you are following and any other activity on your account. Follow a tumblelog by visiting its web pages, and clicking the follow icon in the upper right corner of the page. Alternatively, enter the URL, username, or email of a tumblelog.
- **Add a Text Post**: Insert a comment on a blog or wall post. To foster meaningful dialogue with your community, it is the most essential element to add to a tumblelog.
- **Upload a Photo Post**: Upload any photo through prompts from the website. Photos can supplement other text.
- **Add a Quote**: Enhance your site with a favorite quote or expression to the tumblelog.
- **Add a Link**: Showcase your interests by including favorite websites, blogs and company website to the tumblelog.
- **Add a Chat Post**: Add a dialogue you had with someone or overheard. The example given on the

Tumblr is a chat between an usher and a theatre goer. Here you can use a chat between any two parties.

- **Add an Audio Post**: Enrich your site's offerings with a podcast or another recording from your files. You can also incorporate this feature to embed a recording onto your tumblelog from another website.
- **Add a Video**: Engage your audience by including a video podcast or another video from your files. Or use this feature to integrate video onto your tumblelog from another website.
- **Bookmarklet**: Use this feature to incorporate anything that you find attractive online, including videos, images, music and more. Click on the share on Tumblr bookmarklet, which then tumbles the snippet directly. The result is a varied string of media ranging from links and text, to pictures and videos, and takes very little time and effort to maintain.
- **Feeds**: Import posts from up to five other sites through feeds. In the spirit of original work, if importing other people's content, your account will be suspended.

☼ Tumblr Case Study

"The Signal[63]" is a fashion Tumblr blog with high-quality images and GIF's sponsored by 2014 Lexus. Since Lexus was losing market share with a younger audience, they created the "It's Your Move" campaign, which included images that looked more like a fashion shoot rather than a car commercial. The result, Lexus gained the respect and re-blogs of passionate fashion curators and influencers. This gave new perspective for the brand. "The Signal" has been successful in reaching the targeted audience of 25 – 34 year old's, followed by 18 – 24, which generated more than 4.2 million impressions.

☼ Demographics of Tumblr Users

According to Search Engine Journal,[64] more than 556 million blogs are hosted on Tumblr.

- Most users are between 18 and 29.
- 66% are under the age of 35.

☼ My Observation...

This site is recommended for executives who want to target people under the age of 45 and have little time to blog. I've seen businesses do amazing things on Tumblr including seamless integration between Tumblr and their website. I've also seen companies use Tumblr to promote their products or services by having a blog that is interactive and already has a built-in audience. The site is clean, well-organized, and worth a look. If your buyer persona is part of the Tumblr group, then you should remember to include in your integrated marketing plan.

DO YOU TWEET?

"My favorite social networking site is X because that's the site of choice for people of influence, including journalists. X is particularly important for Newsjacking — the art and science of injecting your ideas into a breaking news story to generate tons of media coverage, get sales leads, and grow business." David Meerman Scott, American Online Marketing Strategist and Author of ***The New Rules of Marketing and PR – How to Use Social Media, Online Video, Mobile Applications, Blogs, News Releases & Viral Marketing to Reach Buyers Directly***, Lexington, MA

The word microblogging comes from X. It's a site with more than 126 million active users,[65] and its Tweeter base is growing every day. It is currently one of the most important social media sites. The site allows you to send and read other updates, otherwise known as tweets, which are text posts of up to 280 characters in length. X is one of my favorite sites because thought-leaders, prominent CEOs, and media people use it regularly to get their message and brand out in the public eye.

On X, I connect with editors and reporters. I post content seeking guest bloggers and recommendations, and I receive them almost instantly. No strings attached!

X allows you to follow people. I like to follow other social media gurus so that I have the opportunity to learn new things. I also follow reporters and editors to find out what types of stories they are working on, and I follow corporations to see how they use X for marketing purposes. Updates are displayed on your profile page and delivered to other users who decide to follow you.

X is used by most organizations and brands, including Cisco Systems, JetBlue, Whole Foods Market, Dunkin', Starbucks, and of course, President Donald Trump.

In addition to the conversation, brands know the SEO value of X. Tweeting with select hashtags can increase your organic reach.

Interestingly, X is so widely used that there is a hashtag, #naturaldisasters that enables residents who use the platform to quickly see what's going on in their area. Government officials also use X to inform its constituents of what's happening in a particular community. One of President Barack Obama's claims to fame is his innovative use of social networking and technology, especially X. Notably, President Obama engaged young people through X, which helped win the 2008 U.S. presidential election.[66] He created a series of tweets that were both inspiring and helped create change.

Here is an example of a tweet posted in February 2018 from President Obama:

"Young people have helped lead all our great movements. How inspiring to see it again in so many smart, fearless students standing up for their right to be safe; marching and organizing to remake the world as it should be. We've been waiting for you. And we've got your backs."

Not only does the government use X to get the word out, but universities and colleges use it too. The University of Texas at San Antonio College of Engineering[67] relays information to students on events at the campus, research, and other student's accomplishments.

When Lance Armstrong[68] lost his bicycle after a significant race in California, he sent out a message via X. Everyone, including the police, saw the message and within hours, his bicycle was found!

Brands and individuals use X every day to get out their thoughts and opinions to share with the X community.

☝ Signing Up

To join X, create a username, which will be available to followers on the site. If later you decide to change the username you can do so without losing the followers, thanks to X's well-thought-out software.

♨ Personalizing Your Profile

Create a profile and upload a photo. This serves as your X icon. Include information about yourself (no more than 280 characters). Stick with the stock backgrounds or change it through the design tab located on the settings tab. Include a link to your blog or homepage. Make the profile public (allowing anyone to follow you), or private (allowing only friends to access your Tweets).

♨ Features on X

On the homepage, there is a stream of various microblogs. Here, you will have an opportunity to either join in the conversation or create a discussion. On the left side of the screen under your username, you will notice the number of people following you and those you are following. Also, if you click on the updates, you will see all of your microblogs.

The @ next to your username is where messages about you are located. The direct messages section is where all of your private messages are located and are only visible to you. The messages sent to @ your username can be seen by everyone on X.

On X, you also have an area to bookmark your favorite Tweet for future reference. If, for example, you saw a post that you would like to keep, add it to your "favorites" section.

There were also trending topics that you can join in to discuss a specific item, for example "Game of Thrones," "Ruth Bader Ginsburg" and "RealDonaldTrump."

And people can easily find real-time resources on X. A writer on "BuzzMachine,"[69] a blog about social media, was on an Amtrack train that stopped moving. He went on X to see if there were updates about the train and learned that there were major delays. Someone else who was on X also microblogged about the situation, and they ended up connecting, getting off the train and carpooling back to New York. He said he even ended up doing business with the person.

I find that when I travel, I use X to ask Delta Assist for updates on travel delays. It works great. I get up-to-the-minute information about the status of the flight.

⸺ Friends

After creating a profile, find and invite friends using X's friend finder. Upload the address book from your email account, and X will find those who are on the site. However, you must select the people you want to follow. Input friends' usernames from other social networking sites, and X will search their database for matches. X provides a URL link so that friends from other sites can follow you. It also appears on Google searches so that people can find you. Post the link in emails and other social networking sites. Friends can be removed from the profile at any time by using the block friend tab.

⸺ Phone Application

Link X to your mobile phone to continue to see your friends' updates as well as post your updates. This gives you the ability to live Tweet and is a great way to communicate about travels. For example, @Whiteonrice linked to a trip they (husband and wife blogging team) took to Vietnam. Every day, they posted new Tweets about their adventures. This helped them increase brand visibility because it offered interest to their followers and generated new fans for their blog, book, and other product offerings.

Whenever I am at the airport or traveling, I also post microblogs about my travels through my phone to show people what I'm doing in the hopes they get to know me better.

☝ What Else Can Be Done With X?

Business leaders can post information about new products or services and link to a website, blog, or media room for further details. They do this to brand their service or product and drive web traffic.

Some people like to share resources on X because it builds their reputation, helps foster relationships, and promotes experts in their field. They post a message and link to an interesting article that they found on the web.

You can also enjoy other activities on X, which are enhanced by the following applications:

- XPro Desktop software so that you can organize your Tweets into columns, such as @replies, direct messages, groups, and keyword searches.

♻ Retweets

A retweet is a post created by one user and then either re-posted by that user or shared with another user. It's important to retweet to make sure an important message is seen.

♻ Interesting People/Companies to Follow on X

- @GaryVee is a social media guru.
- @dmscott an expert in PR and social media marketing.
- @GuyKawasaki is a social media guy and brand ambassador for Mercedes Benz.
- @Scobleizer is a technology enthusiast and blogger that offers a wide range of exciting information focusing on social media.
- @Hilary25 is my username on X (thank you in advance for following me!).
- @HJMT is my PR firm on X.
- @NYLifestyleBlog.
- @ATriDiary.
- @WeRTriathletes.
- @HJMTMedia.

While a wide variety of businesses use X to market products and services, some larger companies, in particular, use X to follow their employees. Their staffers microblog about what they are doing all day keeping the lines of communication open at work.

Many use hashtags before their comment on X to follow a conversation. For example, while watching #GameofThrones, there was a lot of conversation around the topic. It made watching the show more interactive because I was watching not only with my husband, but with my 11,000 X friends.

To search for any topic or company, go to Twitter.com/Explore. You will be directed to a search engine where you can locate any item, organization, or person on X.

Still, others use it to target online media outlets and make them aware of different resources available to them. For example, at HJMT Public Relations, we generate a X pitch, or a "Twich," as HJMT calls it, to the media.

○ Case Studies

X is one of the influential social media sites. Here are a few examples of brands having success on X:

Heinz is known for ketchup, but recently they launched Mayochup,[70] a combination of ketchup and mayonnaise. They did this by launching a poll on X to see if fans would be interested in trying it. Through a series of clever posts, they were able to gain excitement for the new product. In just 48 hours, Heinz got more than 2.4 billion impressions.

Another company that benefitted from X was Dots,[71] a NYC gaming company. Dots used X as a way to drive user acquisitions. They purchased trending hashtags, got retweeted by influential players on X, and they used X to download installs of their app. Interestingly, they created virtual postcards which players could use in the game and that created even more engagement. The game encouraged people to tweet their scores and compete with friends on social. As a result, they earned a Weebly Award and had 30 million players playing the game on X.

⚬ Demographics of X Users

According to Omnicorp Agency,[72]

- 237.8 million users.
- The majority of users are female.
- Majority of the users are between 19 and 49.

⚬ My Observation...

I love X. I highly recommend it. It's a platform that I use every day and keep open all the time. I learn new things on X. I stay in touch with my community, and I conduct business on X by making initial contacts with people and then meeting them in person. I also talk with other people in my field about shared information. The other night I went online and found a conversation about emerging trends in the PR and journalism fields, which I wouldn't have tapped into nearly as rapidly without X.

If X has the right market for you, then remember to include on your integrated marketing plan under the tactics section.

A WORD ABOUT THREADING THE NEEDLE

In today's digital era, brands need to be more than just visible; they need to weave themselves into the fabric of their audience's lives. One way to do this is through the power of 'Threads'. Not to be confused with physical threads, we are talking about digital threads that connect brands to their customers.

Threads are the ongoing narratives or themes that a brand maintains across its digital channels. They are the storylines that keep an audience coming back for more, tying them emotionally and intellectually to the brand. These threads can be anything from a brand's commitment to sustainability, its founder's journey, or the behind-the-scenes process of product creation.

The most effective threads are those that resonate deeply with the target audience. They tap into shared values, interests, or aspirations, creating a sense of community and belonging. For example, a fashion brand might create a thread around ethical sourcing and production, appealing to consumers who value sustainability.

Creating threads requires consistency and authenticity. Brands must ensure that the threads they weave are not only consistent with their identity and messaging but also genuine. Authenticity is key in the digital world, where consumers are increasingly savvy and critical of marketing tactics.

Furthermore, threads should be interactive. Brands can use social media platforms, blogs, and even email newsletters to engage their audience in these narratives. Ask for feedback, encourage user-generated content, or even invite followers to contribute to the thread.

Threads are powerful tools for digital branding. They allow brands to tell their stories, connect with their audience on a deeper level, and stand out in a crowded digital landscape. As we navigate the digital world, threads will continue to play a crucial role in how we perceive and interact with brands.

Remember, it's not just about creating a brand; it's about weaving a narrative that your audience wants to be a part of. In the digital world, threads are not just connecting brands to consumers; they're weaving the future of branding.

☝ Demographics:

- Males make up approximately 68% of the user base, while females account for the remaining 32%.
- Among males, the largest age group is 23-25 years old, constituting 28% of the male user base.
- 11% of males and 5% of females fall within the 18-25 age range.

☝ Observation:

Threads is an attempt by Instagram to streamline intimate sharing and to compete with the rising popularity of other messaging apps. The app allows users to share their camera roll, type out a message, or view their friends' Stories in a more private setting than the main Instagram app. It also has an auto-status feature, which automatically updates your status based on your location, without giving away your coordinates.

While Threads offers a new dimension for more personal interaction, it has been met with mixed reviews. Some users appreciate the focus on more private, close-knit communication, seeing it as a return to the roots of social networking. Others, however, believe it to be just another addition to an already saturated market of social media and messaging apps.

NEEDING HELP ON YELP?

"We find it easy to find customers willing to post positive reviews. Our secret is that we only ask them after we have achieved a successful outcome for them (no other incentives). We do so immediately upon informing them. We also screen happy customers to see if they regularly use Yelp. If they do, then we ask them to post on Yelp. Otherwise, we direct them to other sites." Matthew J. Weiss, Esq., Weiss & Associate, NYC and FL

Yelp can make or break a small business. One bad review and your customers will think twice about whether or not to use your services or buy your products.

Almost every retail business is on Yelp. Many people go to the app or to the site on their computers and look for restaurants, auto repair shops, keys and locksmiths, plumbers, spas and salons and delivery services. They can even make reservations on Yelp.

Yelp is not just limited to retail shops and restaurants. You can also use the site to find hotels, travel, real estate firms, financial services, and even religious organizations.

☼ How Can You Utilize Yelp Organically?

Yelp gets great SEO on Google's search engine. Therefore, if you are on Yelp, you can get a significant return on organic SEO. Your business can certainly take advantage of that. Most of the reviews on Yelp are for shopping and restaurants. However, a small business can also reap the benefits.

One of the most important things to think about with Yelp is to obtain positive reviews, primarily five-star reviews.

Since most customers tend to leave negative reviews on Yelp, it's essential to ask your customers to leave you a five-star review if they are happy with your products or services.

You can do this by leaving a sign in your retail store or you can send personalized notes to your clients asking them to leave a review.

However, if someone does leave a negative review, try not to take it personally. Make sure to respond immediately and try to turn it around.

A good example is a local dress shop on Long Island. They received a negative review on Yelp. They were furious because they started to lose business as a result of that negative comment. They contacted the person who left the comment and the person told them that she was leaving a bad review for a different business. However, the damage was done. CBS-TV picked up the story and contacted me for an interview on what a small business can do when this happens. I said the dress shop should respond to the negative post on Yelp. I also said it was imperative to get positive posts so that the negative one would be lower down on the search. Oftentimes, Yelp will not remove the negative post so the only way around getting the truth out about your business is to get your current customers to help by posting five-star reviews. This will push down the bad review and ultimately, it won't matter as much.[73]

On a different note, Matthew Weiss, Esq. of Weiss & Associates (www.nytrafficticket.com) said, he's been on Yelp for about five years and has more than 200 reviews.

When someone is searching for a traffic ticket law firm in the state of New York or Florida, his company appears high in the search engines on Yelp and on Google. He found that Yelp has increased his business by nearly 6%!

👍 **Yelp Elite Squad**

There are a group of people on Yelp considered Yelp Elite Squad. They get invited to parties, restaurant openings and such because they are "influencers" on Yelp. They do not get paid. However, they are the consumers who continuously post on Yelp giving both positive and negative reviews.

☝ Here Are Some Ways To Become A Yelp Elite Squad Member

1. Create a profile with your real name and photo.
2. Write helpful reviews every time you go to a retail shop or business.
3. Don't stop writing reviews.
4. Have fun with them and let your personality shine.
5. Interact with other elite yelpers. This is a social site after all.
6. Engage with the local Yelp community manager.

☝ Demographics

The social networking site, established in 2004 in San Francisco, CA, has more than 224 million reviews.[74] Here are some other demographics:

- There are nearly 37 million average monthly app users.
- 62% services; 38% restaurants, bars, and retail; with 265 million reviews.
- More than 50% of Yelp users have their college degree and earn more than $100,000.

☝ My Observation...

Most businesses monitor Yelp. Remember, the more positive reviews your business gets, the more likely people will find you and utilize your service. Yelp is also a great way to get organic SEO.

Tip: You may consider targeting elite yelpers and invite them to an event at your business. This could be beneficial to you.

If you have a local business whether it is a retail business or a service business that utilizes foot traffic, Yelp may be the perfect site for you to include in your integrated marketing plan.

WATCH YOUTUBE REGULARLY?

"YouTube has been a reliable host for my videos over the years. Sadly, some of my previous hosting platforms are no longer in business. It's good to know that I can always go to YouTube to retrieve a video and share a link." Steve Garfield, Writer, Photographer, Traveler, Videoblogging, Pioneer, SteveGarfield.com, Boston, MA

YouTube is one of the most popular sites on the internet today. In fact, it is the #2 search engine after Google. Founded in February of 2005, this video-sharing website is used for social networking.

YouTube allows millions of people to discover, watch, and share created videos. It provides a forum for people to connect, inform, and inspire others across the globe and acts as a distribution platform for original content creators and advertisers large and small.

Do You Remember Lonelygirl15?[75]

According to *Wired Magazine*, lonelygirl15 posted videos on YouTube regularly. Every day, she sat in her bedroom and talked about the trials and tribulations of a home-schooled teenager of religious parents. It became one of the most popular videos on YouTube. Later, it was discovered that lonelygirl15 was an actress who graduated from New York Film Academy and teamed up with film directors and a screenwriter. The team succeeded in attracting millions of devotees and coverage in top media outlets, which helped their Hollywood careers. The scenario brings to life how enterprising people can use YouTube to build a following.

However, it's not easy to go viral and for the most part, not necessary. As long as you reach the right target market, that is the goal. If your video teaches something, like a step-by-step tutorial, in my opinion, it seems to outperform those that are talking heads.

YouTube is a user-friendly community. It allows people to easily upload and share video clips both on YouTube, as well as across the internet through other websites, mobile devices, blogs, and email. Viewers watch current events, relive their favorite TV shows, find videos about their hobbies and interests, and discover new artists and filmmakers.

Signing Up

Anyone can sign up for a YouTube account, and upon registration, those who do are given their very own channel.

You can tailor your accounts for branding purposes by:

- Customizing a homepage.
- Changing the playback setup.
- Using the mobile setup to access YouTube by phone or to download the video directly from the phone.

☼ Features on YouTube

You start by uploading a video. Then, you write a title and description of the video and give the video "tags" or keywords that make it easier for people to find. After that, YouTube offers features to enhance the viewing and sharing experience, including:

- Mark videos as favorites.
- Create your customized playlist.
- Search for friends with similar interests. Add them to grow your network.
- Embed the YouTube video on your blog site by copying the URL that YouTube provides in the "share" section. Once you do that, the video can appear on your website or your blog site.

Recently, YouTube came out with a "live" feature, similar to Facebook and Instagram. Here, you can actually record on your mobile phone what is going on at that very moment.

In addition, recording a video from your iPhone is easy and uploads almost automatically. If you download iMovie, you also can easily edit the video before posting.

⚙ What Types of Videos Can You Post?

There are all different types of videos on YouTube, but here are a few that you can utilize for your brand:

- **Tutorial videos** (step-by-step) – for example, how to change a bike tire.
- **Videos that show the back office of your company** – for example, if you are a bakery, you may show bakers actually making the pastries.
- **Educational videos** – for example, this may be where one person provides tips on a particular topic. I did a series of these where I gave insight on my areas of expertise including creating an integrated marketing plan, blogging, pitching editors, etc.
- **Reality videos** – for example, when HJMT recorded Glasslandia, the first Google Glass reality show on YouTube. We filmed six episodes and one blooper episode. Each week, we launched a new show that was similar to the TV show, *The Office*. Through Google Glass, I promoted an associate, hired an administrator and developed a public relations campaign for one of our clients.
- **Interview videos** – for example, you can create a studio in your office and film an interview with someone.

⚙ Demographics of YouTube Users

According to Hubspot,[76] the majority of the users go to YouTube weekly or more and share videos with friends and colleagues. Here are the demographics:

- · 2.5 billion users.

- 90% of the users who watch YouTube are between 18 to 44.
- 377 million are between 18-24.
- 56% of Gen Z, 54% of Millennials, 48% Gen X, and 26% Boomers say they discover new products on YouTube.

☝ My Observation...

YouTube is a great way to get your message out! Companies use YouTube to promote products, services, and happenings. I showcase events we run for clients, press conferences we hold, and highlights from staff retreats. It allows my community to look at what HJMT is doing both inside and out. It is an effective way to market and helps spread your message virally.

Before you create your videos, watch some of the more popular YouTube videos by searching "viral videos." See what the commonality is. What makes them different than other videos? Why do people send them from person-to-person? What would make you send a video to someone else? By answering these questions, you can make a viral video too!

But, remember, it is not about going viral, it's about reaching the right target audience for your business or your brand.

If you think videos will help your business, then remember to include in your integrated marketing plan under the tactics section.

♥ Contests and Promotions

One of the ways to build engagement and awareness for your brand is through the use of social contests and promotions.

These types of promotions can:

- Help you get more engagement.
- Build your email lists or SMS lists.
- Help you go viral if the contest is an experience and fun.

Before embarking on a contest or promotion, make sure to know your audience and hold it where they live on social. It doesn't hurt to experiment with different platforms and figure out what type of contest to run.

According to "SproutSocial.com,"[77] the following type of contests and promotions may be worth pursuing:

- **Campaign using video** - like Facebook, Instagram or YouTube Live. Here, you can host a contest asking your followers to create a video on one of the sites using your product or service. You may even ask them to create a video why they need your service. A few years back, for example, HJMT worked with a local salon and offered a contest for potential customers. The contest called for applicants to submit a video saying why they needed a makeover. The video with the most "likes" was awarded the prize of a full makeover.
- **Comment giveaway** - I find that when I have giveaways, I build a lot more engagement. Here, you

would ask your followers to comment on your blog or
social post for a chance to win a prize.

- **User-generated content campaigns** - Ask your
community to share content, use videos, or live
stream that will get the word out about your product
or service.
- **Tie in with a charitable event** - Millennials love
philanthropic causes so make sure to include a social
cause campaign if that correlates with your brand.

When you give away prizes, make sure they are worthy.
Otherwise, you won't get the participation that you seek.

Make the call-to-action entry mechanism as easy as possible
to get people to participate. If the community has to "jump
through hoops," they will not participate and your contest
will flop.

Another important aspect before you get started, make sure
to jot down the length of time the contest will be held and
where.

Confer with a social media attorney and make sure to
use the proper wording before holding the contest. Proper
rules and regulations need to be in place prior to holding
a contest. Make sure that you follow FTC guidelines and
include disclosure language in your post.

Once you launch the contest, promote as much as possible
and cross-promote on various platforms.

Finally, make sure to evaluate your results.

☝ **My Observation...**

Contests are great but know the rules before holding one. Also, make sure the prize is worthy and that you promote throughout your social networks, blogs, and podcasts.

My firm held a contest for NEFCU Credit Union called, "Season of Giving." Here we asked for non-profit organizations to chip in and share with their followers. They told their followers that if they got the most likes to a post, they would receive $5,000 from the credit union. The contest created a lot of buzz in the community, tons of press coverage, and showed that NEFCU cared about their community by giving back. In addition, we received more than 10,000 followers on social as a result.

If holding a contest or promotion sounds like a good opportunity for you to grow your community with the right market, make sure to jot it down on the integrated marketing plan.

PHOTOGRAPHY — A PICTURE IS WORTH...

"Patience and perseverance — with all of the algorithms and a new community, it helps keep your head together." Jane Pace, Blogger, "Bon Appetit Mom," Long Island, NY

Photography has always been an important component of marketing and public relations. Businesses use photography with a press release or pitch, for press events, and executive portraits.

Did you know that press releases with images get 1.4x[78] more views than those without?

A good photograph is important no matter if you are posting on social or using for a press event.

Here are some tips:

- Make sure the resolution is high quality.
- Don't be afraid to get close to the subject.

- Use action shots rather than staged.
- Try different angles by getting on top of a chair or squatting down.
- Make sure every photograph you take tells a story.
- Don't forget about the background. What's behind the subject? Is it appealing?
- Where is the sun? Don't point directly into the sun, otherwise your subject will get all dark; pointing away will create a better story.
- Look at the composition and make sure it tells a story.
- Start to evaluate good photos on your Instagram or Pinterest feeds and see why they are good.
- Finally, try to be more creative.

There are free sites where you can grab shots but make sure you read all the fine details. If the photographer wants you to credit him/her, then do so. Some of the sites ask for a donation for the photographer. I try to give them a cup of coffee or $1.50 for the use of the photograph. Use your discretion but make sure to abide by what is expected because you don't want to get sued.

Make sure not to use photographs found on a Google search, because although they may not initially be marked, they may be copywritten.

Here are some free sites I would recommend:

- Pixaby.com
- Unsplash.com
- Pexels.com
- PicJumbo.com

I use Photoshop to edit, crop or enhance photos before using on social or on my blog.

♥ The Selfie

Robert Cornelius invented the "selfie" in 1839. However, the word selfie was first tweeted in 2007 and since then has increased in popularity every year.[79]

According to a *Wired Magazine*[80] article, "The duck face, the fish gape, the smize—these are just a few of the time-honored poses that celebrities, influencers, and the Instagram-happy masses have relied upon to create perfect selfies." However, the author writes that a lot has changed and that selfie-takers are now using apps to enhance their appearance or they hire "on-demand photographers through ElsiePic to capture their adventures for them so they can remain 'at the moment.'"

Selfies have become so mainstream that there is even a museum dedicated to it called, Museum of Selfies, located in Los Angeles, California. As the curator said in the *Wired* article, "Selfies are just another form of self-portrait, so saying the selfie is dead is like saying the era of photography is over."

♨ Why do people take selfies?

According to researchers in an article in *USA Today*,[81] there are lots of reasons why people love selfies, including:

- Trying to grab attention.
- Enhance their moods.
- Be more self-confident.
- Social competition.
- Social conformity because others are doing it.
- Selfies can create memories.

Statista[82] shows that more than 60% of all adults over the age of 18 have taken at least one selfie in their lives. 82% of those 18 to 34 have taken selfies; 63% of people between 35 and 54 have taken selfies; and 44% of all 55 and older have taken selfies.

On average, 93 million selfies[83] are posted per day and 10 selfies are posted to Instagram every 10 seconds.

☝ How Can You Use Selfies For Your Brand?

You can create a contest or you can photograph yourself using the product or wearing the product in various locations. At HJMT, we worked with a company that made cookies. We took the cookies to various locations around Long Island and took selfies of us eating the cookie at a park, on the beach, and on the side of the highway. We did this to generate interest for the brand. This helped garner new customers for the cookie company.

👍 My Observation...

Photography has and always will be important. The higher the resolution and the composition of the photograph, the more engagement you will receive. When looking through the lenses of your camera or phone, try looking at the photo differently. Make sure nothing is distracting in the background and that the image pops.

Photography is a must for your integrated marketing plan. Even if you opt not to use any social sites, you will need photography for brochures, newsletters and more. Make sure to include in your plan now.

AUDIO AND VIDEO TO GET YOUR MESSAGE OUT

"Deciding to host my own radio show / podcast has been by far one of my best decisions in business. As the owner of Healy Success Solutions Inc., I consult, train and coach small businesses on how to turn their prospects into profits. So, hosting The Profit Express, where I interview amazing guests who help inspire my target market grow their business, was a perfect match. The benefits of hosting a podcast are incredible. My guests are some of today's most successful experts, entrepreneurs, and industry leaders. These are people I would have never met otherwise. The knowledge and insight they share with my listeners is priceless. That same knowledge has absolutely helped me become a better business owner. And the simple act of promoting The Profit Express keeps me and my company on the minds of my target market each and every week." Tim Healy, Owner, Healy Success Solutions Inc., Host of *The Profit Express*, Long Island, NY

Some businesses will include podcasting as part of their marketing strategy to build their business. Podcasting both in the audio and video realm is vital to include in your integrated marketing plan.

☝ What is a Podcast?

A podcast is an internet radio show that is controlled by you, the consumer. It sounds like a radio show and gives detailed information about a particular topic. It must not be self-promotional. If it is, people won't listen.

As of 2023, there are varying estimates on the total number of podcasts. Some sources suggest that there are over 5 million podcasts globally. In terms of listenership, precise numbers can be challenging to pin down due to the distributed nature of podcast platforms. However, it's clear that podcast listening has been on the rise. According to a report by Edison Research, in 2022, 41% of Americans age 12 and older had listened to a podcast in the last month, translating to about 116 million people. Given the continued growth trend, it's likely that the number of podcast listeners in 2023 is even higher.

Please note that these numbers are constantly evolving as more people discover podcasts and new shows continue to launch.

In *Entrepreneur Magazine,*[85] it said that listeners of podcasts tend to be millennials. With 68 million listeners, 44% are between 18 to 34. They also tend to be educated with 57% holding a bachelor's or graduate degree. More than half of the people listening to podcasts are listening in the car and

40% are listening when they are active like walking, running or riding a bike.

Podcasts help generate viral marketing. Use podcasts on an RSS feed, on iTunes, on your website, and other aggregators.

For Hilary Topper on Air, I pay Libsyn.com to host my podcasts and distribute to iTunes, Google Play, SoundCloud, Apple Podcasts, Amazon Alexa and more.

Compelling podcasts feature a spokesperson, whether an articulate staff member or the owner, discussing the company, product, or service. Each week you can record a new introduction and end with a teaser, inviting listeners to stay tuned for next week's podcast. Having a voice behind your product or service is vital to connect with future consumers.

Podcasts don't have to be polished. There is something about ones that are authentic because they instill trust. Try to strike a balance between casual and professional.

When formulating a podcast, it's crucial to have an outline or a script to keep you on target. It's helpful to put some music in the background based on the type of industry and podcast subject. There is a host of free music online. Explore and determine which one suits your podcast best. Music keeps the interview on pace and on track. It also helps to keep the listener focused on the discussion.

♻ How to Make a Podcast

First, think about a plan of action. Ask yourself the following questions:

- What is the theme? Who am I trying to attract?
- How long will it be? How often will I record?
- What is my unique opening and closing?
- Will I have a call-to-action at the end?
- Should I interview guests, or should it just be my opinion?
- If I interview guests, how will I find them? What questions will I ask?

A podcast can be easily produced with an MP3 recorder, a lavaliere microphone, and some editing equipment. Editing software can be found free on the internet. One popular software on the market is called Audacity, but you can also use Garage Band, which is frequently found on Macbooks. I use iMovie and then convert the file from a MP4 to a MP3.

Think about the location where you will record the podcast. Do you want to record at the office with the background noise? Moreover, if you do, will that add to the charm of the podcast?

Sometimes the best spot to record a podcast is in your closet (if it's big enough). The clothes will muffle the echo and the sound quality could be on point.

Editing does take time, so be patient. It could take a few hours, and a few tries to get it right. In addition, you may consider taking out all the "umms." However, I like to leave them in. I find that the "umms," make the podcast seem more real and spontaneous.

Once you finalize it, it's time to post. However, before that, you need a hosting site. There are a lot out there that offer unique opportunities. Some are free hosting sites, while others charge a nominal fee. Make sure to check out Podbean, Libsyn, Blubrry or BlogTalkRadio.

After finding a host and producing the show, now it's time to promote. Make sure to have an RSS feed on your website so that people can subscribe. Promote the new show via email, social networking sites, blogs, or you may even consider sending a press release to a local newspaper.

The more listeners, the better, and the more you include podcasts into your social media marketing program, the higher your SEO ranking will be. I try to promote the episode when it comes out via social networking sites. Then, a few months later, I repurpose the podcast on my blogs. In addition to that, I send out an email, once a month to my community of more than 10,000 people to let them know new podcasts are available.

♂ Video Podcasts

According to Hubspot,[86] more than 1 billion hours of video are uploaded to YouTube every minute and one billion hours of video are watched every day.

YouTube, Vimeo and other online vehicles that showcase videos are all the rage right now. This is because people like to watch people in action. Video podcasts are potent tools for getting a message out. They can appear on all of your social networking sites, and like television, they draw the viewer in. The best video podcasts are those that are raw and authentic. Polished podcasts don't cut it because they look professionally done, and they tend to be unbelievable because they look too much like commercials.

Before you start, think about what type of video you will make for YouTube. Will it be a solo video of you talking about your passion? Will it be an interview-style, instructional video, or a series?

Next, you may want to purchase an inexpensive camcorder. When I first started to do video podcasts, I spent around $3,000 for a proper camera that had high definition quality. However, podcasters can now use their iPhones or Android devices to film. The quality today is outstanding. Remember to flip your phone sideways so that you fill up the screen.

When you film, think about b-roll. That's the supplemental footage needed to create a story. Always film more than what you think you will need.

☝ Editing

Download the iPhone or Android MP4 onto your desktop for editing or, you can edit right on your phone. I use a few different editing apps for my phone including iMovie, but there are a ton on the market. Go to the app store or the Google Play store to find one that is right for you. For my desktop, I use iMovie because it's free and easy to use. But, if you don't have a Mac, you can download Movie Maker, which is also free but not as robust as iMovie. Some of the paid-for editing software on the market include Final Cut Pro and Premiere. These have a bit of a learning curve but once you understand how to use them, they will provide you with various tools to enhance your video efforts.

Editing is the tricky part. It requires a lot of time and patience.

Jump cuts have been a popular way to edit videos in recent years. The trend before that was on transitions. Now, you will see a lot of hard cuts. This adds to the interest of the video and keeps the viewer focused.

There are endless possibilities to incorporate into a video. Some use these podcasts as a video log or vlog, which they record regularly. These are "blogs" for YouTube. To see an example of a vlog, go to YouTube and put in vlog in the search. Quite a few vlogs will appear on your page to review.

Brands use videos to promote a product, contests, or upcoming event. Some use them to get a message out to the community; for example, a superintendent of a school district may talk about school updates to parents.

Video is a very engaging medium. Consider Skype, free software that allows you to make phone calls over the internet and at the same time, view live video feed. Why are these so popular? Because people want to see the person they are listening to or talking with. It's more engaging, and ultimately, I suspect these will gain more popularity as time goes by.

I also like to use Zoom.us. You pay for the service, but it works well for both audio and video podcasts. It records to the cloud and is easily downloadable.

⚫ My Observation...

Podcasts and video podcasts are essential in every social media plan. When made right, they help create viral marketing and get your product or service noticed. At HJMT Media Company,[87] we have an audio podcast launched once a week.

Many companies have succeeded by using audio and video podcasts. Blendtec is a great example. As a result of their videos, sales went up 700% as noted earlier.

Another great example was one in which HJMT was involved. We produced a series of videos for our client, LI STEM HUB. The videos focused on unique and interesting jobs for high school students to explore. The goal was to share various types of professions with the grade school students and also let them know that there are unique jobs on Long Island. Each video had a different theme. One video focused on the Massapequa Preserve and what environmental engineers do there. Another focused on how surf boards are made and where composites come from. As a result, the videos did so well that we were nominated for an Emmy Award!

One thing to remember is, you must do something different and be creative to get people to watch.

If podcasts and/or video podcasts are right for your brand, include in your integrated marketing plan.

IS DIRECT MAIL AND EMAIL MARKETING STILL RELEVANT?

"Direct mail can be a powerful way to send your message to your target audience. It can show your creativity, introduce new products or services via samples or discount codes, and can also remind people about your overall brand. Now that email has become the norm, the right direct mail campaign can make your business stand out from the rest." Lisa Gordon, Executive Vice President, HJMT Public Relations, Inc., Boulder, CO

How many pieces of mail do you get? What about email?

If you're like me, you get very little mail and lots of email, mostly junk email. So, what happens to the junk email? It gets deleted. But is email marketing dead?

No!

☝ Direct Mail

Today, with the prevalence of social media, traditional direct mail is sometimes overlooked but it may be worth taking a look again.

Direct mail can be creative and can integrate with your social media marketing approach.

Before embarking on a direct mail approach as one of your tactics in your integrated marketing plan, consider the following:

1) What are you selling?
2) What are you trying to accomplish?
3) What's your call-to-action?
4) Who is your audience?
5) Where do they live? Demographics?
6) What would appeal to this group?

Then once you've answered those questions, think about different ways to get your message across. Bob Stone,[88] a direct marketing guru and author who passed away in 2007, suggested that you incorporate one of the following into your campaign:

- Have a yes/no offer.
- Make sure you have an offer with a time limit.
- Include an offer with a free gift especially when the gift closely matches your prospect's interests.
- Sweepstakes usually increase order volume, especially for impulse items.
- Get people to have emotion.

- Put the piece in an envelope as opposed to just sending a postcard.
- Make sure to include a call-to-action.

The thing about direct mail is you can be as creative as you like. For example, I purchased dozens of miniature people and set them up as if they were at an event. I photographed the people and generated a postcard. Once the postcards were printed, I took the miniature people scrambled them up and put them in a box with the postcard. The postcard said, "let us organize your next big event." The campaign had a great return on investment, as it didn't cost that much to produce, and we landed a large job as a result.

☞ Email Marketing

Email marketing isn't dead either. Today, email marketing is done a little differently than in the past. It's about stories. People want to read a story. They don't want to be sold to. They want to be inspired and that inspiration will turn them into customers.

There are several different hosts today including Mailchimp, Constant Contact, and Target Marketing.

"Copyblogger.com"[89] gave these suggestions:

- Make your emails personable. Write as if you're emailing one person.
- Email when you have something valuable or helpful to say.
- Act as if you are a friend.

- Be clear if you want sales messages to be incorporated into your email marketing.
- Empathize and ask how you can help.
- Share a useful tip.
- Let your enthusiasm and personality come through.
- Mix up your greetings to make the email more personal.
- Make sure to add your personality and write informally.
- Write short, strong sentences and get to the point quickly.

☝ Statistics

What I like about Mailchimp or any of the other email services is you get to see how many people opened your emails, how long they stayed and if they shared any information. You also get to see if there was any conversions on the part of your buyers.

☝ My Observation...

I like to incorporate both direct mail and email marketing into the whole integrated marketing plan. They both play an important part of the puzzle. If using them creatively, you can certainly gain market share. If you feel that either or both tactics should be included in your integrated marketing plan because they will tap into your buyer persona, then include them now.

GOING VIRAL!

"Going viral sounds great. But, it is overrated and hard to plan for. Instead, focus on building a core audience that truly engages with you. That's not easy either, but with steady work and engaging content, you have a good chance of success." Sree Sreenivasan, Former Chief Digital Officer of New York City, Met Museum, Columbia and Loeb Visiting Professor at Stony Brook University, NYC

These days, everyone wants to go viral, believing that it is the best strategy for selling more products or services. For years, we developed publicity programs that would create a snowball effect. For example, when we held an event, we would send out press releases at least six to eight months before the event and then every month after that. A month before the event, we sent out information weekly. This would generate coverage from the media.

Going viral means ensuring that a product or service appears on the internet in many different places, including blogs, podcasts, video podcasts, and multiple social networking sites. It's more than just getting millions of views on YouTube. You need to make sure that you are reaching the right target market at the right time.

☼ What Makes Something Go Viral?

It is the re-blogging, the sending of podcasts and video podcasts to your community and the forwarding of information from social networking sites. Going viral also means that people put your blog or information in a social bookmarking spot and share it with others. Soon, hundreds of thousands of people read about your company and get excited about your company's offerings.

Burger King[90] is a great example. They came up with the idea of marketing the aroma of the flame-broiled burger as a men's cologne. They launched the cologne and within weeks, they sold out. After that, the cologne was only available on eBay for no less than $20, when it originally sold for $3.99. Bloggers, online journalists, and social networking people all wrote about this cologne, posting links to the product. Whether or not they thought it was a good idea didn't matter. Their action created demand.

About a month later, Burger King announced on Facebook that if you de-friend ten friends on Facebook, then you would receive a free Whopper. Why? They wanted to see how much their supporters loved Whoppers. Thousands of people took Burger King up on their offer and received coupons for a free Whopper. It didn't take long. One person saw it, blogged about it, tweeted about it on X, sending the information out to a whole group who sent it out to their community and so on and so on. That's what viral marketing is all about.

Another excellent example is of a service going viral. My favorite is the infamous Ice Bucket Challenge[91] developed by ALS (Amyotrophic Lateral Sclerosis). The challenge was to pour a bucket of ice water over your head and challenge your friends to do the same. This campaign made more than $115 million!

☝ Why Did It Go Viral?

For starters, it kicked off in the summer. There was celebrity participation which helped spur much interest. Finally, the campaign was done for a cause.

☝ My Observation...

Anything could go viral with the right idea and the right celebrities. Anyone can also make a video or a social media campaign. But not every idea will go viral. If you seek that, then you may want to reach out and recruit influencers or celebrities to help you launch your idea. Otherwise, does it matter how many tens of thousands of people see your video or your campaign? Shouldn't it only matter if the right people, the people who will pay you for your product or service see it?

A WORD ABOUT DIGITAL ADVERTISING

"A solid digital marketing plan is pivotal. This should include a combination of social media marketing, search engine marketing (SEM) and search engine optimization (SEO). Many people ask me what the real difference is between SEM and SEO. The best way I can describe it is to think of your business like a garden. SEM is like a watering hose, and SEO is like the rain. You can turn SEM on and off at your discretion, and if you want more water (customers) you can turn on the water or even buy a bigger hose (increase your ad spend). SEO on the other hand is only partially in your control. You can make your garden as rain friendly as possible and it still won't rain. Just like you can optimize you site for a special keyword, but people may not search for the particular term." Kyle Finneron, Owner, Finn Performance, Pittsford, VT

Advertising in newspapers, magazines and on television or radio may still work. But today, the majority of the advertising dollars are spent online.[92] There are various places in which

to advertise including Facebook, LinkedIn, Pinterest, and YouTube, to name a few.

Each has its relevance, and each targets its communities. What's interesting about digital advertising is that you can zone into the exact demographic that you want to focus on, and those ads will appear in front of that group.

It's important to note that I'm only going to touch on some of the aspects of advertising on these platforms, and a whole book can be dedicated to this topic.

☼ What is the Difference Between Organic and Paid for Search?

Organic search is achieved when a consumer types something into Google and your name and company are found. Paid search is the same thing, except that you can guarantee that you are on the first page of Google.

Tips on having a good digital advertising campaign:

- Have a clear call-to-action.
- Make sure to have a compelling message.
- Use landing pages to track your results.
- Don't forget about the imagery.
- Test, monitor and then test again. Nothing is fool proof. What works for one company may not work for you. A smart marketer once said to me, "test, test and test again." Once you find something that works, stick with it until it doesn't work anymore.

☝ Native Ads and Sponsored Content

A native ad looks like it is part of the online source. For example, you will see a cruise ship photo on Instagram and it looks like a regular post. However, it will say sponsored ad above or below it and that's how you know it's an advertisement.

Sponsored content looks like it's part of the editorial coverage but is paid for by the advertiser.

☝ Banner and Display Ads

These can be purchased on certain online publications or blog sites. It has your ad and a link back to your website.

☝ Google Ads

When you determine your long tail keywords, you can use these keywords for Google Ads. Remember, people search in terms of a question, like, "where is the nearest coffee shop?"

When you buy Google Ads, you pay for the ads in terms of clicks. Every time someone clicks on your ad, you get charged. How much you pay per click and your quality score (which is the relevance of your ad to your website), depends on your positioning on Google.

You can bid a certain amount per click and you can also set a budget as to how much you are willing to pay per day for the ad.

An impression is how many people see your ad but don't click on your ad.

A conversion is when someone clicks on your ad and you get a concrete result from that click. That result would be a hire, someone retains you, or a sale.

☝ **My Observation...**

Google Ads is a great tool to use when you are not getting organic results from your website or blog site. Make sure to use those long tail keywords in your copy for optimized reach. Google Ads can get expensive, but if you need quantity in your business, then Google Ads may be for you.

If you only have a business page on Facebook, you may not get the reach you are seeking. With the algorithms changing every day, many people who may follow your business on Facebook, may not see your posts. Therefore, it could be beneficial for you to boost your posts or take ads out on Facebook to build up your audience.

It may make sense to take out an Instagram, X and Pinterest ad as well to grow your community. The algorithms make it nearly impossible to grow organically.

If you feel that digital advertising will help increase your brand awareness, then make sure to put in your integrated marketing plan.

NON-PROFIT ORGANIZATION'S ROLE IN SOCIAL MEDIA

"We have found that social media is an excellent way to increase awareness of the Theresa Alessandra Russo Foundation (www. theresafoundation.org) and our activities such as the Theresa Academy of Performing Arts, Theresa's Fun Place (an adaptive playground), and the many events we host to benefit children with special needs. By posting on X, Facebook, Instagram, and LinkedIn, we have been able to extend our reach beyond the New York area and cultivate a following nationwide. Social media has also become an important and effective part of our fundraising efforts. Finally, we have found social media to be more cost effective than traditional media." Vincent J. Russo, Esq., Founder, The Theresa Foundation, Long Island, NY

Social media and non-profit organizations go hand-in-hand. It allows the organization to promote its mission, reach its community, communicate with donors via the internet, and reach many new constituents.

In many instances, non-profits, in their quest to support a cause, are so pressed for time and resources, they are not able to pursue all of the latest avenues available to them. Still, just as with a small or large business, a non-profit organization needs to build a community.

There are many ways to do this, and I talk about this in previous chapters, but the most effective way to launch a social media campaign is to have one person or outside provider, spearhead the effort.

The reason to have one person start the effort is to speak in a focused voice the community will recognize. It also helps to coordinate the massive community-building effort that the non-profit organization must undertake before going forward with the social media plan.

Moreover, as your organization adds more people to your community, you will be able to better build your brand and reputation because by getting the word out to one, it will likely spread to others. By building your audience, your organization will quickly have thousands of followers receiving information about your cause and upcoming events. Best of all, those who do implement social media campaigns find that a strategy is an excellent tool for driving traffic to the organization's website, building buzz, recruiting volunteers, raising money, and further supporting their work.

♻ Getting Followers and Friends

One of the most time-consuming efforts is trying to find followers and friends within your social networking sites.

This is time well spent. Use it to carefully identify and select the most suitable locations and search various groups on these sites that correlate with your mission. On some of the social networking sites, like X, you can even segment the market by zip code, demographics, and interest using www.Twitter.com/Explore. For example, say you have a health organization, and you're interested in what people are saying about the flu, go to www.Twitter.com/Explore and type in the flu, and you will find a group of people talking about the flu.

If your board members have accounts on any of your targeted social networking sites, make sure that they help you build your community. Ask them to send out notices to their friends and followers to join your page. Also, if the organization has petitions to sign or is accepting donations, board members can send out notices to their friends and followers to support the cause.

Don't forget to utilize your staff members. They all have followers and they can encourage them to follow your brand too. However, you may need to provide them with an incentive to do this. Don't just count on them sharing information after hours.

Remember to keep up the effort. Building a community takes time and patience, but it is the best way to get your message out to the right people.

♨ Building Awareness

Why should a non-profit organization have a page on Facebook, X, Instagram, and/or LinkedIn?

Social networking allows the non-profit to gather a community together to help build their brand awareness and visibility for a cause. People are genuinely interested in causes and issues. They want to hear what an organization is doing and see if the charity is worth pursuing. Social networking can spread the latest news about a non-profit and its most recent achievements. Some use it to announce a new video that highlights the organization's good work, such as a newly built school or distribution of a much-needed vaccination to a third world village. What better way to inspire new supporters?

☝ Targeting Bloggers

What is another way to gain brand awareness for your non-profit? Conduct an online search and identify bloggers who are interested in your position and cause. Asking them to help you by writing a story or posting to their social channels about your organization. Even when unsolicited, bloggers are often happy to support worthy causes. For example, people who I don't know have asked me to post stories for them on my blog. Once I hear their stories and research them to make sure they are legitimate, I am happy to write a blog entry about various issues that matter to me.

Getting bloggers to tell your story is a great way to continue to get the word out on the internet as potential supporters will more readily find you. Make sure that bloggers link your site to their blog. This will help you move up on the search engines.

Consider sponsoring blogs as a form of advertising. It's inexpensive, effective, and the linkbacks will help you generate new potential donors.

♂ Real World Fundraising Efforts

By engaging an audience, non-profit organizations can help build up their fundraising efforts. Here are some examples of grassroot organizations:

♂ XRoads NYC[93]

There are more than 1.5 million people hungry in NYC. XRoads NYC is an organization dedicated to alleviating hunger. The group created a campaign where they used chalk-drawn faces in the places where the homeless congregated. They wanted to make consumers aware that being homeless on the streets and eating off the streets was not a "pretty site." The project goal was to generate awareness and help eliminate hunger. XRoads NYC took this art and posted on Instagram. By doing so, they were able to raise $1.4 million dollars. Xroads NYC used some of the donations to create more exposure with signage and posters. They exceeded their goals by generating more than 63% more donations, a 20% increase in volunteers, and a 50% increase in donated groceries. More than 156,000 meals were served. Xroads NYC won a Shorty Award for this campaign.

♂ Love Has No Labels[94]

Another excellent example of a non-profit campaign, which also won a Shorty Award, was Love Has No Labels, a non-profit organization dedicated to inclusion. The group installed a live x-ray machine on Valentine's Day in Santa Monica, California which showed an x-ray of two people, in some cases more, dancing. When they came out from behind the x-ray machine, the viewers saw members of the LGBTQIA community and people of color. The purpose of the video was to demonstrate that we may look different on the outside but we all look the same on the inside. To gain greater visibility, the video, that was created at the event, was shared on social.

From the video and live event, Love Has No Labels, had more than 10,000 attendees and garnered more than 40 million views on YouTube.

☝ Other Strategies for Non-profit Organizations

When charities and non-profit organizations post audio and video podcasts on the internet about their causes, they help boost awareness and viral marketing for their brand. Supporters often also post podcasts on social networking sites, helping to spread the word about the good works of their favorite charities. Furthermore, organizations should consider pitching stories to online publications. Once these articles are published, organizations can better highlight their cause and at the same time, improve their search engine rankings.

☝ My Observation...

Non-profit organizations, like small and large businesses, need a strategic integrated marketing plan to accomplish their goals. Be sure to set a policy in your organization for users of online media. Also, have one department, preferably your PR department, handle the task of building a community and creating content about your organization. If you don't, you can have lots of people spreading messages about your brand in different ways, making the message inconsistent and not credible. This form of viral marketing is not the kind that you, as an organization, want!

DEALING WITH NEGATIVE POSTS?

"From a legal standpoint, if someone writes a bad review about your company or its product or services, you may be able to take legal action against them for defamation if the review contains false statements that are injurious to your business and its reputation. If the review, however, is not defamatory and reflects statements of truth or the reviewer's opinion, then legally it is protected speech. Another potential avenue, however, may be the platform itself. Depending upon the social platform on which the review is posted, the platform's terms may provide an avenue for recourse or takedown of the review under certain circumstances. It also bears noting that the federal Consumer Review Fairness Act protects a person's ability to share his/her honest opinion about a business's products or services in any forum, including social media. In so doing, the Act prohibits a company from using a gag clause in its consumer contracts, including in its online terms and conditions, which would allow the company to sue or otherwise penalize consumers for posting a negative review." Terese L. Arenth, Partner, Moritt Hock & Hamroff LLC, Long Island, NY

What happens when someone writes a negative tweet about you on X? Alternatively, an angry customer posts a nasty blog about your company on his blog. What happens if these negative posts go viral?

For starters, you must monitor everything about you, your company, and your employees. My favorite free web-monitoring tool is Google Alerts, but there are many others available. There are lots of paid-for services as well. Do your homework and make sure to get one that will work for you.

The downside of Google Alerts are 1) you don't always get an alert and 2) users do not receive the alerts instantaneously. Google Alerts enables you to track comments, posts, and anything else where your name, company name, or employees' names appear. Another great search tool is Twitter.com/Explore. This enables you to search on X for your company, name, or anything else of interest. It will also tell you who made which comment so you can view their profiles on X.

Once you see an angry response or something written negatively about your company, it is tempting to react. However, take it from a PR pro, don't overreact. Think twice before responding. Look at the source, overall reach and whether you have the opportunity to shift the conversation to a positive. Consider the tone in your voice. If you want to say something, come across intelligent and not angry. Please don't ignore it. Respond without getting defensive.

There are times when negative things are said on Yelp or Google, and they are not right. Respond to clarify the misinformation and correct the record.

How do you get rid of those negative reviews? You don't. However, you can push them down on the search results. Get folks to write positive things about your business. Ask your satisfied customers. Ask your staff. Ask your vendors. The more positive reviews on both Google and Yelp, the better.

One of the businesses we represent on Long Island had negative reviews on Yelp. They were a plumbing company and wanted the post removed. The post was untrue and they called Yelp for help. Since Yelp wouldn't do anything, we discussed several options and ended up strategizing and getting their customers who were thrilled with their service to post positive reviews. Between responding to the misinformation and the positive reviews, this brought down the negative review and kept the plumbing business thriving.

We live in a world where reviews count. If there is a negative review of your business, it doesn't matter how hard you work; you need to address it.

To me, the anonymous negative reviews are bogus. If you can't respond to a real person then who is to say that the person who wrote the negative review isn't your competitor. Competitors have been known to do worse things to hurt your business. In that case, get positive reviews to push it down.

♻ How Do You Start?

My suggestion would be to develop a crisis communications plan for social media. The sooner you do this, the better. According to Hootsuite,[95] first come up with a social media policy, which will include:

- Creating guidelines for copyright, privacy, confidentiality, and the voice of the brand. (All too often many people are the brand, and the voice isn't the same. It should be consistent.)
- Make sure all your passwords are secure. When an employee leaves, change your passwords.
- Make sure to have a social listening program in place. In addition to Google Alerts, use Hootsuite Insights, where alerts can notify you as soon as they happen. ZeroFOX, another Hootsuite product, also does the same thing by sending you alerts on offensive content, malicious links, and scams targeting your business. Tweetdeck is another product used to monitor X.

Then, when developing the plan, include:

- Have a chain of command. Delegate roles of each person and/or each department.
- Determine who will be the spokesperson.
- Develop a list of FAQs and have them on standby.
- Write up some tweets.
- Do a drill and figure out what was good or bad about it. Make sure to do this a few times.
- Pause all marketing efforts until the crisis is resolved.
- Address the issue directly without being defensive. Refrain from arguing.
- If all else fails, call a social media expert or a social media attorney.

♥ *"Social media can be a handy platform to promote a company's business, product, or services, given its viral nature and the opportunity for real-time engagement with consumers and building brand recognition. Clients frequently use social media for promotional marketing campaigns like sweepstakes and contests, as well as influencer campaigns; however, while practical marketing tools, social media promotions, and marketing are not without potential legal risk. They are governed by a myriad of laws and regulations and are also subject to the same rules and regulations that apply to traditional media and promotions. These laws and regulations may include, by way of example, the lottery laws, privacy, and data security laws, the Federal Trade Commission Act (governing unfair and deceptive trade practices), the FTC Guides Concerning the Use of Endorsements and Testimonials, and intellectual property laws. In addition, most social media platforms have their promotional guidelines in which to be adhered. Businesses conducting social media promotions must be cognizant of the relevant legal issues and are advised to consult with their attorney to protect themselves from potential exposure to liability."* Terese L. Arenth, Partner, Moritt Hock & Hamroff, PC, Long Island, NY

☝ **My Observation…**

Social media is the fastest way to get your message out and heard. It goes hand-and-hand with crisis intervention. I believe that all businesses that are in the public eye need to be on the internet. It is essential more now than ever before to incorporate a crisis intervention plan. Response to a situation is key. Make sure to include a crisis plan with your integrated marketing plan.

SOCIAL MEDIA IN AN AGE OF FAKE NEWS

"Fake news - what to do about it? Here's what I do about it. 1) I acknowledge that is exists, 2) Fact check, fact check, fact check. Check against several reputable sources. If they say the same thing, likely not fake news. 3) The minute you spot fake news, call it out, and ask your community to stop sharing the fake news. Try to find out the true story, and offer that. 4) Encourage your favorite news sources to work hard to combat fake news. Support their commitment to journalism as a high calling. Pay money for good news. Do you know what is real? What is fake? If enough fake stuff is posted in your feed, does that make it real?"
Imei Hsu, Citizen Blogger, www.myallergyadvocate.com/blog, Seattle, WA

Fake news is a "real" thing and a real problem! According to a Pew Research Study,[96] "Americans rate it as a larger problem than racism, climate change, or terrorism."

♻ What Exactly is Fake News?

Fake news is the spread of news that is not real. Governments, corporations, or individuals can spread fake news because they want to get people to display emotion, or take an action as a result of this false information you believe is true.

For example, how often have you heard that a celebrity died when he is still alive? Or, remember the story of a homeless man giving his last $20 to a woman in need of gas money? The woman then went on to start a GoFundMe campaign to raise money for the homeless man. She raised $400,000 as a result and ended up going to jail because she spent all that money herself.

♻ What Can People Do About It?

The Pew Research study says that many people find that fake news or what they call "Made Up News," stems from politics. People they surveyed say they don't blame the journalists. Most people are aware of the fact that fake news is always around us. They take precautions and fact check various posts they see on social media.

♥ Social Media Attitudes Changed Significantly, But Not That Much!

When I got into social media in 2006, people looked at me as if I were an alien. Today, more than 69%[97] of all adults are involved in social media. Now, many businesses from tiny mom and pop shops to large corporations have a presence on Facebook, X, LinkedIn, Instagram, and Pinterest.

In 2011, HJMT Public Relations conducted a survey that asked our community if they had a social media plan in place; most said they did not. However, 75% of those questioned had a Facebook page. According to Hootsuite,[98] there are now more than 80 million small and medium business pages on Facebook.

We also questioned our community about their attitudes on bloggers versus reporters. We found that 40% of those who answered the survey trusted reporters more than bloggers, and 14% trusted bloggers more than reporters, with nearly 50% not sure whom to trust.

We asked our community recently, and this time, the answers were a little different. Twenty-nine percent said they trust reporters more, while 21% said they believe bloggers more. Interestingly, 52% still said they were not sure whom to trust.

When asked if our community reads blogs online, a substantial majority of 87% said they do and that 65% read at least 1 to 5 blogs a day. The majority (65%) read blogs that focus on news, but lifestyle (51%) and health (35%) were close behind. Most of the respondents read blogs because they have a thirst for more knowledge in a particular area.

The majority (75%) of the people questioned were business owners who don't target bloggers in their outreach efforts. We found this interesting since having bloggers as brand ambassadors or as a place to publish a guest blog entry aids in the search engine optimization process.

Since I last published my book more than 10 years ago, small and large businesses have embraced social media but some still have not acknowledged bloggers in their social media/public relations strategies. Those who are forward-thinking and include bloggers in their plans will be ahead of the pack just like those who were on Facebook in 2009.

Now, if you don't have an Instagram page, a Facebook page, or a X handle, you missed the boat. Even businesspeople who don't understand social media, know that it is essential and will hire someone who knows how to post but may not know how to develop a social media marketing strategy. Be wary of doing this. It's not going to do anything for you if you don't have a plan of action.

☝ My Observation…

When you see something that doesn't look right, make sure to double-check it for yourself before spreading or sharing it with your community. The more people become proactive about this, the less likely there will be "fake news." Journalists and consumers need to take this responsibility and make sure that when something is shared, it is accurate and not false.

LIKE

LIKE IT OR NOT, WEARABLES ARE HERE TO STAY

"Think about 10 years ago, can you imagine that we would be as tech wise as we are today? So, where will we be 10 years from today? Your imagination can run wild and much of what you think, will probably happen." Peter Goldsmith, Chairman, LISTnet, Long Island, NY

According to Statista, the wearable tech market made an impressive debut, securing more than $49.6 million in market share. However, that was just the beginning of a technological revolution. Year after year, this burgeoning industry has continued to exceed expectations, growing exponentially in both popularity and profitability.

In the early days, wearables were seen as a novelty—fun gadgets that could track your steps or monitor your heart rate. But as the technology advanced, so did the applications. Today, wearable devices have evolved into essential tools that play a significant role in health monitoring, fitness tracking, communication, and entertainment.

The global wearable technology market, valued at $61.30 billion in 2022, has shown no signs of slowing down. In fact, it's quite the opposite. Analysts predict a compound annual growth rate (CAGR) of 14.6%, indicating a rapidly expanding market. By 2026, the wearable technology industry is expected to exceed a staggering $265.4 billion, according to Markets and Markets.

This impressive growth can be attributed to several factors. The development of 5G technology has significantly boosted the capabilities of wearable devices, allowing for faster data transfer and more complex applications. Furthermore, the increasing consumer demand for sophisticated devices that can seamlessly integrate with their daily lives has fueled the market's expansion.

From smartwatches and fitness trackers to virtual reality headsets and smart glasses, wearable technology is redefining how we interact with the world around us. It's not just about convenience or staying connected; it's about enhancing our abilities and enriching our experiences.

Yet, this is just the tip of the iceberg. As the market continues to grow, reaching an estimated $419.44 billion by 2028 according to Mordor Intelligence, the possibilities for wearable technology are virtually limitless. With advancements in AI and machine learning, future wearables could offer even more personalized and immersive experiences.

As we look to the future, one thing is clear: wearable technology has forever changed the way we live, work, and play. And with its continued growth and development, the best is yet to come.

Wearable technology is more than just a trend, it's a significant shift in how we interact with technology, our environment, and even ourselves. Here are some reasons why we should care about it:

Health Monitoring: Wearable devices like fitness trackers and smartwatches can monitor vitals such as heart rate, blood pressure, sleep patterns, and physical activity. This information can help individuals maintain a healthier lifestyle, and it also opens new possibilities for remote patient monitoring in healthcare.

Convenience: Wearables offer the convenience of hands-free operation. Whether it's checking notifications, making phone calls, listening to music, or getting directions, wearable technology allows us to do these tasks without needing to reach for our phones.

Improved Productivity: In the workplace, wearables can improve productivity and safety. For example, smart glasses can provide workers with real-time information or instructions, allowing them to complete tasks more efficiently.

Data Collection: Wearable tech collects valuable data that can lead to personalized insights and recommendations. This data can be used in areas ranging from health and fitness, to understanding consumer behavior, to enhancing employee performance in the workplace.

Potential for Innovation: The growth of wearable technology is driving innovation in numerous fields, including fashion, entertainment, healthcare, and more. As the technology continues to evolve, it will open up new possibilities that we can't even imagine yet.

In conclusion, wearable technology is reshaping our world in many ways. By integrating technology more closely with our daily lives, wearables have the potential to enhance our health, increase our productivity, and transform the way we interact with the world around us.

☝ **My Observation:**

Wearable technology is a rapidly evolving field that is increasingly becoming a part of our everyday lives. These devices, which range from fitness trackers to smartwatches, are designed to be worn on the body and serve various functions, enhancing convenience, productivity, and health monitoring.

The popularity of wearables is driven by their ability to seamlessly integrate technology into our daily routines. They allow us to track fitness metrics, receive notifications, manage schedules, and even make calls hands-free. This level of accessibility and convenience is changing the way we interact with technology, making it more personal and intuitive.

Moreover, the future of wearable technology looks promising. As advancements continue, these devices are expected to become more sophisticated, offering even greater functionality and personalized experiences. The development of smart glasses, for instance, opens possibilities for augmented reality applications, potentially transforming industries such as entertainment, education, and manufacturing.

Furthermore, the data collected by wearable devices offers valuable insights into user behavior and health, which can lead to improved products and services, as well as advancements in healthcare.

In conclusion, wearable technology is not just a passing trend, but a significant shift towards more integrated and personalized technology use. Its growing popularity indicates a future where technology is not just something we use, but something we wear and interact with in a much more intimate and seamless manner.

The wearable market is expected to expand exponentially and knowing this, we as marketers can adjust accordingly.

Does wearable tech and IoT belong in your plan? If so, take a moment and add it to your tactics section.

WHERE DO WE GO FROM HERE? WEB 5.0

"Web 1.0 focused on information, access to it, via the new Superhighway and thus organized search was the war ground to produce dominant players; 2.0 started marketplaces & platforms, like eBay, Myspace, Facebook & LinkedIn... interactivity & community was its war ground, and produced its dominant players; 3.0 furthered marketplace & platforms but focused on mobile tech & location presence and so Waze, Uber, Lyft, Instagram & WhatsApp flourished (Facebook adapted with Messenger); and, 4.0 will be about IoT, including biotech (from wearables to bioembeds, like Elon's latest announcement)... AR/VR is this war ground, where AI, machine learning & bio enhancement are all merged into various tech platforms, business models, products & companies. While Oculus, MS HoloLens, and NeuraLink fight it out with what Alexa, Samsung, & Watson will become...we don't know yet. However, I'm looking forward to becoming bionic!" Vikram Rajam, President, Practice Marketing, Inc., "Videosocials.net," Long Island, NY

Web 5.0, while not yet fully realized, is projected to be a paradigm shift in how we interact with the internet. This new era, often referred to as the "emotional web," is anticipated to create an environment where technology can interpret and respond to human emotions. It also promises a more decentralized platform that empowers users to gain control over their data and identity.

The cornerstone of Web 5.0 is the integration of artificial intelligence (AI) and machine learning technologies into regular internet usage. The aim is to make the web more intuitive, responsive, and personalized. Essentially, Web 5.0 will use AI to understand user needs better, predict their behavior, and provide tailored outputs, creating a seamless, personalized online experience.

Web 5.0 is also expected to enhance our connectivity by fostering a more inclusive and accessible internet. With AI and advanced algorithms, the web could become more adaptable to different languages, cultures, and abilities, thereby bridging digital divides, and promoting global inclusivity.

Moreover, Web 5.0's emphasis on decentralization could revolutionize how we handle data and privacy. By leveraging blockchain technology, Web 5.0 could enable peer-to-peer transactions and interactions without the need for intermediaries. This shift could give users more control over their data and potentially disrupt traditional business models.

However, the transition to Web 5.0 also brings challenges. Ensuring security in a decentralized environment, managing the ethical implications of AI, and maintaining user privacy are just a few of the issues that need addressing. It's also crucial to ensure that this evolution doesn't exacerbate digital inequalities but instead promotes digital inclusivity.

Web 5.0 is still in its early stages, it promises to transform our digital connectivity dramatically. By making the web more intuitive, personalized, and decentralized, Web 5.0 could change how we interact with the internet and each other. As we move towards this future, it's essential to navigate these changes responsibly, ensuring a web that is accessible, inclusive, and beneficial for all.

☝ **My Observations:**

As we stand on the brink of another seismic shift in our digital landscape, I have been closely observing the emerging discussions around Web 5.0. While it's not yet fully established, there are several key trends that seem likely to shape its development.

- **Artificial Intelligence and Machine Learning**: Web 5.0 is expected to integrate artificial intelligence (AI) and machine learning technologies more deeply into our online experiences. This could lead to a more intuitive, responsive, and personalized web, with AI algorithms interpreting our needs and predicting our behavior to provide tailored outputs.
- **Decentralization and User Control**: Web 5.0 is projected to be a more decentralized platform that gives users control over their data and identity. By leveraging blockchain technology, it could enable peer-to-peer interactions without the need for

intermediaries, disrupting traditional business models and shifting power dynamics on the web.

- **Emotional Connectivity**: Often referred to as the "emotional web," Web 5.0 aims to create an environment where technology can interpret and respond to human emotions. This could transform our relationship with the digital world, creating a more empathetic and human-centric internet.

- **Greater Inclusivity**: With advanced algorithms and AI, the web could become more adaptable to different languages, cultures, and abilities. This has the potential to bridge digital divides and promote global inclusivity.

However, alongside these exciting possibilities, there are also significant challenges ahead. Ensuring security in a decentralized environment, managing the ethical implications of AI, and maintaining user privacy are all critical issues that need addressing. Moreover, it's crucial that the evolution towards Web 5.0 doesn't exacerbate digital inequalities but instead contributes to a more inclusive and equitable internet.

While at the publishing of this book, we're still in the early stages of Web 5.0, these observations suggest a future where our digital connectivity is transformed. It's a future that holds both exciting opportunities and significant challenges - and one that we must navigate responsibly to ensure an internet that benefits all.

LASTLY, BUT NOT LEASTLY...

I want you to take out that integrated marketing plan that you've been working on while reading this book. Now make sure that the following elements are included in it:

Goal

Objective

Strategies

Target Audience

- Who is it that you are targeting?
- Demographics?

Tactics

- Graphic Identity
  - What will you develop?
  - Will it reflect your brand?

- Blog
  - How often?
  - Topics?

- Social Media Marketing
  - Which sites will you use to reach your target audience?
  - How often will you post?
  - What time of day?
  - What will you post?
  - Will it attract your buyer?

- Podcasting
  - Audio? Video? Or Both?
  - How often?
  - Content?

- Public Relations
  - Should traditional PR be incorporated into the plan?
  - What publications will you target?
  - What types of pitch letters or press releases will you produce?

- Direct Mail and Email Marketing
  - Should you incorporate into your plan?
  - Do you have mailing lists?
  - Do you have something that you want to share?

- Data Visualization and Photography
  - What will you use to help get your message out?

- Contests and Promotions
  - Should you have a contest or promotion?
  - Will that help you reach your goal?

- Experiential Marketing
  - Should you create an event that will help you reach your goals?

- Would it be beneficial to you to have your target audience meet you?

- Wearable Technology or IoT
  - How will you incorporate into your marketing program?
  - Should you include?
  - What if you don't incorporate?

- Crisis Plan

- ROI – Return on Investment
  - Did you get a decent return?
  - What was it that you were anticipating?

We have included a sample plan on our website, at www. hjmt.com/BrandinginaDigitalWorld for your review and to get an idea of what an actual plan looks like to compare with your plan.

👍 My Final Observation...

We have just walked you through the process of branding yourself and your company. We have also showed you how to take that brand and market it to your selected community. Remember none of this is a science. As marketers, we do everything through trial and error. So, try out what you think will work for your brand. If it works, great. If it doesn't, try something else. Remember, you've got this and if you are consistent and keep it up, you will be able to pursue your passion!

Good luck! And remember, my door is always open. You can tweet me at @hilary25, or find me anywhere else on social by typing HilaryTopper. Thank you for reading!

GLOSSARY

"I'm a B2B player and we've shifted our content strategy to use Linkedin first, and rewrite/capsulize it for your blog. Previously one might not of thought of LinkedIn as social media, but it actually has become that." Kenny Schiff, Founder & CEO, CareSigh, NYC

Artificial Intelligence (AI) refers to the simulation of human intelligence processes by machines, particularly computer systems. These processes include learning (the acquisition of information and rules for using the information), reasoning (using rules to reach approximate or definite conclusions), and self-correction. AI is designed to enable machines to perform tasks that would normally require human intellect such as recognizing speech, making decisions, translating languages, and identifying patterns. Rather than operating under a specific set of instructions, AI systems are trained using data, allowing them to improve performance as they are exposed to more information. This technology is used in a wide range of applications, from voice assistants like Siri and Alexa, to recommendation algorithms used by streaming services like Netflix or Spotify, to autonomous vehicles, medical diagnostics, and much more.

☍ Augmented Reality

Augmented reality is an experience that a user has where objects that are not in the "real world" look and feel as if they are in the real world. These images are projected via computer and sometimes they include not only visuals but also audio and scent senses as well.

☍ Algorithm

An algorithm is a formula set by each social networking site or by search engines that changes periodically for relevancy and user experience. It's essential to keep an eye out for articles and research on algorithms because this is how your company can maximize its placement on Google search.

☍ Avatar or Bitmoji

An avatar or Bitmoji is an image or photo that you would use to represent your online presence in a social networking site.

☍ Blogging Platforms

A blog is a weblog or online diary. Some bloggers talk about their personal lives or businesses, while others blog about specific topics. There are industry-related blogs, for example, blogs about social media and marketing. There are blogs about any topic you could think of including niche markets, such as fishing, golfing, running, dieting, and more. Blogs also help build a community by creating interesting posts where people can comment and get a conversation started. Some blogging platforms include WordPress, SquareSpace, Wix, Weebly, and Blogger.

☝ Blog Directories

If you are looking for a blog on a specific topic, several directories can help you find exactly what you seek. Some of these directories charge a fee, so check the site carefully before using.

☝ Bookmarking

Just like flipping the corner of a page on a physical book, bookmarking enables you to mark a web page that you find important, so you can access it at a later date. There are many different bookmarking services that are free. Just Google it.

☝ B-Roll

B-roll is typically used in news when a reporter is discussing a subject, and the station shows visuals of what the reporter is discussing but the viewer only hears the reporter's voice. For example, if the reporter is talking about the railroad, you will see a photo or video of the railroad and just hear his or her voice describing the railroad.

☝ BuzzSumo

Ever wonder what content is shared the most? Buzzsumo will tell you, and you can use this information to pitch the media because it will enable you to see what is trending and what a reporter or editor would find relevant.

☝ Call-to-Action

A call-to-action is a step that someone can take when prompted. For example, at the bottom of your website, you would have your phone number, address and email for further contact. That would be considered a call-to-action.

☝ Cision

Cision is an online database that tells professionals where to find reporters and producers. The beautiful thing about this database is that you can compile a list of contacts from anywhere in the world. To make the most of this database, know your target audience, geographic reach, and the beat. It's important to sift through this list and do your homework.

☝ Chat Rooms

Chat rooms are places where people go online to find others with common interests. There are many different types of chat rooms found throughout the internet. To find a list of various chat rooms, search a specific topic, and multiple options will come up on the search engine. The difference between chat rooms and forums or message boards is that they take place in real-time getting you instantaneous responses.

♂ Community

On all social networking sites, it's essential to have a community, and the only way to have one is to create it either organically or through advertisements. The goal is to garner people who have similar interests or ideas and bring them together to form a community. It is also imperative that the community's members interact with one another. Be strategic in figuring out ways for this to happen.

♂ Content Aggregators

Several good content aggregators will enable you to push out your content to several different social networking sites and schedule them at various times throughout the day. In the past, I've used Buffer, Sendible, and Hootsuite, but several others are excellent products and worthy of the time to investigate.

♂ Conversion

This is when someone sees something online or in print and then buys something as a result.

♂ CPI (Consumer Price Index)

The US Dept. of Labor Statistics defines CPI, consumer price index, as a measure of the average change over time in the prices paid by urban consumers for a market basket of consumer goods and services.

☼ Crisis Communications

Crisis communications is deployed during an anticipated or serious event, where a CEO or publicist responds by either protecting or defending the person, product or company whose reputation is threatened.

☼ Email Providers

There are many email providers on the market. For a small fee, you can create high-quality HTML emails to send to your community. I've been using MailChimp, but you can also check out Constant Contact, HubSpot or Target Marketing.

☼ Emoji

These are the little symbols that people use in either posts, blogs, emails (in the subject line) or even as a response to someone else's post. You've seen them. They could be a heart, a happy face, or several different graphic images that reflect what you're thinking or feeling at the moment. Sometimes, emojis are stronger than words. They can depict a general emotion or an emotional response to something specific. Facebook and many of the other social sites have incorporated emojis into their mix. Instead of "liking" something that someone posts, you can now show a "sad" or a "wow" emoji.

☼ Friends and Followers

The people in your social networking community are often referred to as friends and followers. Each social networking site calls these people something different. For example, on Facebook, they are called friends, on LinkedIn, they are called connections, and on X, they are called followers.

☝ Google Alerts

Everyone should have a Google Alert set for themselves. If you have a client, set the alert for the client's name, business, and industry. This way, every time something is written on the web, you will see it. It doesn't hurt to also set up a Google Alert on your competitors or your brand subject area.

☝ Google Analytics

There are many different ways to get your analytics for your website. The most popular method is through Google Analytics (GA). Here you can find out what your readers like, who they are, where they come from, and other interests. Other ways to get analytics is on your actual website through Webalizer and other popular sites. Your Google Analytics tells you lots of information about your blog or website. You get to see your audience's interests and who they are in order to tailor your message. You can use Google Analytics to see how people are visiting your blog or website. Where do they come from? How old are they? How often do they visit? What are they interested in? What town are they from?

☝ HARO

Help A Reporter Out (HARO) is a free service for both reporters and publicists. Reporters or producers post what kinds of sources they are seeking and publicists reach out to connect with them. It's an excellent service and a valuable resource for anyone in the business.

⟳ Hashtags

A hashtag is a symbol used on social networking sites to annotate a word or phrase. When you hashtag something, you insert the "#" in front of the word. Hashtags can be tracked. So, for example, if you are interested in running the NYC Marathon and want more information on it, search "#NYCMarathon," and everything written about the NYC Marathon will appear in a stream. There are a few ways to find popular hashtags. The easiest way is to type the hashtag in the search box on Instagram or X. There, you will see if the hashtag is popular or not. The more popular the word or phrase, the more people will see your post.

⟳ Impressions

An impression is when someone sees an ad, a post, a blog article, an online publication, etc. that focuses on your product or service on the internet or in print.

⟳ Influencers/Ambassadors

Many smaller companies find that setting up a blog ambassador program makes financial sense. Ambassadors promote the brand and either get paid or get swag in return.

☝ Infographics

Everyone loves photos, and infographics are the next best thing. They enable you to take the results that you gathered from a survey and put into an exciting visual format that your consumers will enjoy reading. There are several free sites that you can use. My favorite is PiktoChart. It's simple to use, free, and enables you to make an attractive graphic for your audience.

☝ Internet Forum or Online Message Board

Internet forums or online message boards are where people with common interests get together and post messages. Questions are asked and answered by those involved in similar situations, in a non-real time discussion group.

☝ IoT

IoT or the Internet of Things is a term used to describe how smart products interact with each other and with your mobile device, oftentimes as a hub.

☝ Jump Cut

Instead of using transitions to go from one scene to another, jump cuts are hard breaks in a video. Although they are "choppy," they work and are popular among podcasters.

◌ Keywords

Keywords are words or phrases that describe your brand. It is advisable to have approximately 10 "long tail keywords," meaning 10 terms that could appear in your website, social networking sites and blogs in order to help you rank higher in the search engines. Using these keywords on a consistent basis will help you get organic search results.

◌ Meta Tag

Meta tags are code that tell the search engines what your website is about.

◌ Microblogs

Microblogs are mini-blogs or status updates, also known as content, posted on any social networking site. Many social networking sites have their own terminology for a status update. For example, on Facebook, one would say a microblog would be a status update. On X, it would be called a Tweet, and on LinkedIn, it would be called a post. Microblogs are the common phrase for anything related to preparing a post or update that would appear on your site.

◌ Muck Rack

Muck Rack is a website that connects PR professionals with journalists. Here, PR people can view X feeds and learn what journalists are writing about. This way, PR professionals can tailor their "pitch" when presenting story ideas.

☝ Online Newsrooms

Online newsrooms are becoming more and more popular. It's a place to host your press releases. Remember to keep your statements SEO ready, so that people searching can find you. Online newsrooms also enable you to share the release with your social community.

☝ Pitch Letter

A pitch letter is a short, succinct letter that enables you to provide enticing information to help the media understand what you are selling. Public relations professionals use pitch letters to entice the media to write about their clients.

☝ Plugin

A plugin is like an app for your website. It enables you to enhance and customize your website. Plugins need to be added to a website, as they are not included in its content management system. Some plugins are free and others you have to pay for, similar to an app for a mobile device.

☝ Podcasts

Podcasts have gained so much popularity in recent years and continuously grows. Podcasts are radio shows recorded through the internet, and can be listened to anytime, anywhere.

☼ PicMonkey

PicMonkey enables you to resize photos or create collages and share on social media.

☼ Return on Investment (ROI)

ROI means the ratio between net profit and the cost of investment. A high ROI means that your return is higher than what you put into it.

☼ Real Simple Syndication (RSS)

RSS feeds allow you to receive information via a feed aggregator like Feedspot. Feedspot takes all of the RSS feeds from blogs, news sites, YouTube, podcasts, and so on, and puts them in one place. The RSS feed enables you to read all of this in one location. You can also send RSS feeds to your email list.

☼ Re-Tweet

This is when you share something with your community that you like or find interesting that someone else wrote on X. When you share, it's called a re-tweet.

☼ Selfie

These are photographs of the photographer, taken by the photographer, typically on a mobile device.

☝ Slack

Slack is an internal/external chat room in real time. Similar to instant message, Slack is easy to use, and you can have a live discussion with clients and staff.

☝ Shortened URL

Software like TinyURL, Bit.ly, among others, is used to shrink long URLs that you can then use in a post. Go to one of these sites, paste in the long URL, click on the link and you will then get a shorter version, which visitors to your site will find much easier to use. These shortened versions also track the number of users clicking on the link. This will provide you with accurate analytics as well.

☝ Social Listening

Social listening are generally tools that monitor social media, blogs or anything else that is written about your company online.

☝ Social Networking Sites

Social networking sites are online sites where you can build communities in which you can also exchange dialogue. All social networking sites are very similar. Most feature a place to post your status, where you can then have conversations with friends and followers. You also have an opportunity to post photos and videos, and can share a bit about your personal life to help make connections.

☼ Search Engine Optimization (SEO)

SEO is a process for getting a website, blog, or anything else on the internet to appear higher up on the rankings of popular searches engines, including Google.

☼ Social Bookmarking

Social bookmarking is a way for you to store, manage, organize, and search for web pages. There are sites where you can store articles that you want to save in one place. There are other social bookmarking tools where you can actually tag something that you think is interesting and then it will be ranked in your own bookmarking system.

☼ Survey Monkey

Survey Monkey is a helpful tool when trying to develop a story for your audience. This free tool enables you to create surveys and then analyze results. The paid version provides many additional features, and if you plan on using this for research, the paid version is the way to go.

☼ Trends

It is essential to keep up with things that are trending – topics that everyone is talking about and sharing perspectives. It's important to keep up with trends because it helps you to know how to position your brand in the current environment. For example, we represented an air conditioning company. When there were articles about a heat wave coming, we were able to place the owner on CBS-Radio talking about tips to keep you cool in the summer. By checking out the trends, we were able to develop the story. You can find these topics through Google Trends, X Trends, and even Facebook Trends. It's important to see what's trending to see where your brand fits in.

☝ Tweet

A Tweet is a status update used specifically on X. It is 280 characters or fewer and can reflect the mood, a feeling or just a message that you want to share with the community at large.

☝ QR Codes

QR (quick response) codes are two-dimensional bar codes that can be scanned using a smartphone. QR codes, once scanned, will automatically direct someone to a website, blog, or social networking site. Today, businesses are using them to give special consumer discounts or offers on products or services. They are also used to provide consumers with more information.

☝ Waze

Waze is a crowd-participation site and mobile app that enables you to use it as a GPS for directions, see where police are hiding, find out where stopped cars are and if there are any accidents. The service also helps you determine the fastest route to a particular destination.

☝ Webmap

A webmap is a guide that helps you organize your website. Here, you can sketch out on paper what you think you would like included in your website.

☝ Wikis

Wikis are web pages that allow individuals to update or add information to the page. For example, Wikipedia is the online encyclopedia that enables anyone to input information on just about anything. Wikipedia has become the online source to get free information. Years ago, it was Encyclopedia Britannica; now it's Wikipedia, written by consumers like you.

☝ Yammer

Yammer is an internal site owned by Microsoft. It enables you to talk with someone in your office or someone in another office in real time.

☝ Zoom.us

Zoom.us enables you to hold meetings and webinars online. You can have up to 100 people in the meeting at one time. Zoom.us is becoming more popular these days than Skype.

ACKNOWLEDGMENTS

There are many people that I would like to thank for their help and support with this book. First and foremost, I want to thank my family for their love and support. My daughter helped me edit the book even when she came home late from work, my husband proofed it, and my son always encouraged me. I appreciate their help and am grateful to have them in my life.

I also want to acknowledge my dad, Herbert Mass, for teaching me that persistence is a virtue and the way to get things done. My brother, Ed, and his family for cheering me on in business and triathlons. My cousin, Mindy, who is my absolute soul sister and sounding board. My mother-in-law, Marilyn, for inspiring me to always do better.

Special thanks to my confidant and business partner, Lisa Gordon who, without her, I would have never been able to get through this.

Also, a big thank you to my Hofstra students who ask me thought-provoking questions, my blog readers, my running club, my triathlon team and to my community at large – everyone on X, Facebook, LinkedIn, Instagram, Pinterest, etc. I greatly value your insights and learn from you every day. Thank you for your love and support!

I am truly grateful! xoxo

AUTHOR'S BIO

Hilary JM Topper, MPA, has more than 30 years of public relations, advertising, and marketing experience. In March 1992, Hilary founded HJMT Public Relations, a boutique NY Public Relations and Social Media Marketing Agency.

Before HJMT, Hilary was the Director of Public Relations and Development at Professional Service Centers for the Handicapped, Inc. (PSCH). In 1989, Hilary Topper joined Ruder Finn Public Relations where she was the account executive for Jell-O and GLAD Wrap Bags. She represented clients on broadcast media and implemented a grass-roots fundraising campaign in local markets.

Prior to that, Hilary was the Director of Public Affairs and Development at Altro Health and Rehabilitation Services. She was responsible for the day-to-day public relations, marketing, and fundraising activities. In 1985, Hilary worked at Hill, Holliday, Connors, Cosmopulos, Inc., Public Relations as an account executive. There, she handled the PRESTONE II antifreeze account, coordinating a national radio promotion. Also, Hilary managed The National Community Gardening Contest, sponsored by the American Community Gardening Association. She also trained spokespeople for media and placed them on national and regional television.

Before that, Hilary worked at Ogilvy & Mather Public Relations. There, she worked on Dove Beauty Bar, Quadro (a children's construction kit) and Kinder-Care Learning Centers. Hilary wrote press releases, pitch letters, and booked media tours in local markets. Before that, she worked at CLAIROL, Inc. publicizing hair care products and at Public I Publicity, promoting musicians and music books.

Hilary has received numerous awards and honors for her accomplishments within the industry from PRWeek, Long Island Business News, Newsday, Girl Scouts of Nassau County, the Communicator, International Association of Business Communicators, Long Island Center for Business and Professional Women, Fair Media Council, "DiversityBusiness.com" and the Stevie Awards.

She is an Adjunct Professor at Hofstra University and has taught there for more than eight years. Subjects she taught include Digital Communications, PR Tools, Media, Messages, and Messengers, Persuasive Presentations, and PR Campaigns.

Hilary is a published author and has given numerous speeches and seminars across the country. Her first book, ***Everything You Ever Wanted to Know About Social Media,*** was published in 2009, she also wrote **From Couch Potato to Endurance Athlete – A Portrait of a Non-Athletic Triathlete** in 2022.

Hilary is also blogger and podcaster. Her blogs – HilaryTopper. com and A Triathlete's Diary Blog have won numerous awards and recognitions. She also has a podcast, Hilary Topper on Air, which helps people grow personally and professionally.

In her spare time, she coaches WeREndurance.

She received her Bachelor of Science degree from Hunter College and her Master's in Public Administration from Baruch College.

FOOTNOTES FOR BRANDING IN A DIGITAL WORLD

1   Topper, Hilary JM, "Everything You Ever Wanted to Know About Social Media, but were afraid to ask…" 2009
2   Klara, Robert "How Sony's Walkman Changed the World" Adweek, March 2015 https://www.adweek.com/brand-marketing/cds-mp3s-little-machine-made-music-portable-163469/
3   Hootsuite press release, January 26, 2022, Hootsuite.com/newsroom/press-release/digital-2022report
4   Gray, Glenn "Why public relations agencies are evolving," Forbes online, July 2017 https://www.forbes.com/sites/forbescommunicationscouncil/2017/07/21/why-public-relations-agencies-are-evolving/#2b36d96717f4
5   Schwantes, Marcel "A New Study Reveals 70% are Actively Looking for a New Job." Inc. Magazine, December 2018 https://www.inc.com/marcel-schwantes/a-new-study-reveals-70-percent-of-workers-say-they-are-actively-looking-for-a-new-job-heres-reason-in-5-words.html
6   Kusinitz, Sam "The Definition of a Buyer Person (in 100 words)," Hubspot Blog, April 2019 https://blog.hubspot.com/marketing/buyer-persona-definition-under-100-sr
7   Lake, Laura "What is Integrated Marketing and Why is it Important" The Brand, Small Business Blog, June 2019 - https://www.thebalancesmb.com/what-is-integrated-marketing-and-why-is-it-important-2295739

8   New World Encyclopedia, Ivy Lee, March 2018 https://www.newworldencyclopedia.org/entry/Ivy_Lee

9   Mostegel, Iris "The original influencer," February 2016 https://www.historytoday.com/miscellanies/original-influencer

10 Clement, J., "Number of monthly active Facebook users worldwide as of 2nd quarter 2019 (in millions)" Statista.com, https://www.statista.com/statistics/264810/number-of-monthly-active-facebook-users-worldwide/

11 Gallucci, Nicole, "French Inventor Flies across English Channel on a Jet-Powered Hoverboard" Mashable, August 2019 - https://mashable.com/article/french-inventor-franky-zapata-crosses-channel-hoverboard/

12 Edwards, Luke, "7 Wearables to Look Out for in 2019" Techradar, December 2018 https://www.techradar.com/news/7-wearables-to-look-out-for-in-2019

13 Youtube, Ft. Myers & Sanibel "Find Your Island Challenge on the Beaches of Ft. Myers & Sanibel" September 2013 - https://www.youtube.com/watch?v=Vo96VxzM_4A

14 Youtube, "First Google Glass Reality Show - Glasslandia Episode 1, October 2013 https://www.youtube.com/watch?v=oJRQ7tmbHog&t=83s

15 HilaryTopper.com, http://www.hilarytopper.com

16 McLuhan, Marshal "Understanding Media: The Extensions of Man," published in 1964

17 Mainwaring, Simon "The New Power of Consumers to Influence Brands," Forbes, September 2011 https://www.forbes.com/sites/simonmainwaring/2011/09/07/the-new-power-of-consumers-to-influence-brands/#358ff5953b3c

18 Laptop Magazine, https://www.laptopmag.com/ 2008

19 Anderson & Jiang, "Teens, Social Media & Technology 2018" Pew Research Center, May 2018 https://www.pewinternet.org/2018/05/31/teens-social-media-technology-2018/

20 http://www.WeRTriathletes

21 http://www.teamgallowayli.com

22 Onibalusi, Ayodeji, "What Defines High-Quality Links in 2019 and how to Get Them?" Search Engine Watch, May 2019 https://www.searchenginewatch.com/2019/05/07/how-to-get-high-quality-links/

23 Bulluck, Lisa, "These are the Biggest SEO Trends of 2019" Forbes, January 2019 https://www.forbes.com/sites/lilachbullock/2019/01/10/these-are-the-biggest-seo-trends-of-2019/#231fa8615805

24 Toonen, Edwin, "What is Googles Knowledge Graph?" Yoast blog, May 2019 https://yoast.com/google-knowledge-graph/

25 www.ATriathletesDiary.com

26 Becker, Branden "11 Examples of Experiential Marketing Campaigns that will give you Serious Event Envy" Hubspot Blog, https://blog.hubspot.com/marketing/best-experiential-marketing-campaigns

27 Benjamin, Kim, "Coca-Cola Hosts AR Experience World Cup" Campaigns, June 2018 https://www.campaignlive.co.uk/article/coca-cola-hosts-ar-experience-world-cup/1485768

28 Kim, Jiwon, "Refinery29 Takes Experiential Marketing to Another Level" PSF.com, September 2017 "https://www.psfk.com/2017/09/refinery29-experiential-marketing-another-level.html"

29 AdAge, "Volkswagen: Fun Theory Piano Staircase" https://adage.com/creativity/work/fun-theory-piano-staircase/17522

30 Wikipedia, https://en.wikipedia.org/wiki/Social_networking_service

31 http://www.HilaryTopperonAir.com

32 http://www.HJMT.com

33 Sutter, Collier "KFC Sent This Amazing Portrait to The X User Who Spotted Their 11 Herbs & Spices Joke" https://people.com/food/kfc-twitter-following-spice-girls-herbs/

34 Blendtec Youtube Channel, "Will it Blend" 2018 https://www.youtube.com/channel/UCnFP0IU4gpnmcLnVzDLUtfw

35 Case Study: Reach Robotics, Youtube, December 2018 https://www.youtube.com/watch?v=Td2AXEtGAxc

36 Statista, "Number of Bloggers in the US from 2014 – 2020 (in Millions), February 2016, https://www.statista.com/statistics/187267/number-of-bloggers-in-usa/

37 Zantal-Wiener, Amanda "A Brief Timeline of the History of Blogging" September 2016 https://blog.hubspot.com/marketing/history-of-blogging

38 Harshorne, David "WordPress Vs Blogger: Which Blogging Platform Is Right For You?" Blogging Wizard, September 2019 https://bloggingwizard.com/wordpress-vs-blogger/

39 http://www.SethGodin.com
40 Jeff Bullas Blog, "Why blogging makes you trusted and credible," - https://www.jeffbullas.com/why-blogging-makes-you-trusted-and-credible/
41 Blogher, http://www.blogher.com
42 The Social Network, https://www.imdb.com/title/tt1285016/
43 Facebook Newsroom stats https://newsroom.fb.com/company-info/
44 Omnicore blog, Facebook Facts, September 2019 - https://www.omnicoreagency.com/facebook-statistics/
45 O'Kane, Caitlin "A photo of an egg is the most-liked post on Instagram, beating record held by Kylie Jenner" January 2019 - https://www.cbsnews.com/news/a-photo-of-an-egg-is-the-most-liked-post-on-instagram-beating-record-held-by-kylie-jenner/
46 Instagram Blog, https://business.instagram.com/blog
47 OmniCore Blog, "Instagram by the numbers" September 2019 https://www.omnicoreagency.com/instagram-statistics/
48 Wix Blog, "The Most Popular Instagram Hashtags You Should Know" July 2018 - https://www.wix.com/blog/2018/07/popular-instagram-hashtags
49 Fitzgerald, Brittany "11 Instagram Tips For Beginners: Etiquette Rules Every User Should Know" June 2012 https://www.huffpost.com/entry/instagram-tips_n_1557614?guccounter=1&guce_referrer=aHR0cHM6Ly93d3cuZ29vZ2xlLmNvbS88&guce_referrer_sig=AQAAABxRVXjzyQc8yNoY8vygiqKB3vXFet28PN2cloRoV_-otl_7pipuyUym2iX6HhFoauW_dP4v3IldEn3rUM6Ov1mnrXnIvu-Y0gU1ZxczXMxV-ZS49VRQ7jw0GEyTR9eius3PnDFLIQbkV5CL1hs4DHOKEc9un78p5HNxOruSwjVV
50 Worthy, Paige, "Top Instagram Demographics that Matter to Social Media Marketers" Hootsuite Blog, September 2018 https://blog.hootsuite.com/instagram-demographics/
51 Kirkpatrick, David, B2B Social Media Marketing: DocuSign's targeted LinkedIn InMail strategy creates 3 large pipeline opportunities" May 2013 https://www.marketingsherpa.com/article/case-study/docusign%E2%80%99s-targeted-linkedin-inmail-strategy
52 Hibbard, Casey, "How LinkedIn Brought $72,000 in Sales for PostcardMania," November

2011 - https://www.socialmediaexaminer.com/
how-linkedin-brought-72000-in-sales-for-postcardmania/
53   OmniCore Agency, "Linkedin by the Numbers: Stats,
     Demographics & Fun Facts" September 2019 https://www.
     omnicoreagency.com/linkedin-statistics/
54   Piombino, Kristin, "Honda's Shoestring
     Pinterest Campaign Attracts Millions," PR Daily,
     February 2013 - https://www.prdaily.com/
     hondas-shoestring-pinterest-campaign-attracts-millions/
55   OmniCore Agency, Pinterest by the Numbers: Stats,
     Demographics & Fun Facts, September 2019 - https://www.
     omnicoreagency.com/pinterest-statistics/
56   Feiner, Lauren, "Reddit users are the least valuable of any
     social network," CNBC, February 2019 https://www.cnbc.
     com/2019/02/11/reddit-users-are-the-least-valuable-of-any-social-
     network.html
57   Sattleberg, William, "The Demographics of Reddit: Who Uses
     the Site?" TechJunkie, July 2019 https://www.techjunkie.com/
     demographics-reddit/
58   OmniCore Agency, "Snapchat by the Numbers: Stats,
     Demographics and Fun Facts," September 2019 https://www.
     omnicoreagency.com/snapchat-statistics/
59   Sloane, Garett, "BMW Test Drives Snapchat Lenses in First
     3-D Car Ad," AdAge, November 2017 https://adage.com/article/
     digital/bmw-test-drives-snapchat-lenses-car-ad-3d/311394
60   Snapchat Blog, "Fitbod sees 31% lower cost per acquisition on
     Snapchat"
     https://forbusiness.snapchat.com/inspiration/
     fitbod-sees-31-lower-cost-per-acquisition-on-snapchat
61   Hootsuite Blog, "What is TikTok, Who Uses it, and Should
     Brands Care About it?" May 2019 https://blog.hootsuite.com/
     what-is-tiktok/
62   Bump, Pamela, Hubspot blog, "How 7 Brands are Using
     TikTok" September 2019 "https://blog.hubspot.com/marketing/
     brands-on-tiktok"
63   Loke Hale, James, "Jimmy Fallon's TikTok Parntership
     Resulted in Record Engagement Spike for App"
     November 2018 https://www.tubefilter.com/2018/11/20/
     jimmy-fallon-tiktok-the-tonight-show-partnership/

64 Shorty Awards, "The Signal" Lexus Tumblr Winer, 2014 https://
shortyawards.com/6ᵗʰ/the-signal-lexus-tumblr

65 Costill, Albert, "50 Things You Should Know About Tumblr,"
January 2014 Search Engine Journal - https://www.
searchenginejournal.com/50-things-know-tumblr/84595/

66 Shaban, Haza, "X Reveals its Active Users Numbers for
the First Time," February 2019, Washington Post, https://
www.washingtonpost.com/technology/2019/02/07/
twitter-reveals-its-daily-active-user-numbers-first-time/

67 Bogost, Ian, "Obama was Too Good at Social
Media," The Atlantic, January 2017 https://www.
theatlantic.com/technology/archive/2017/01/
did-america-need-a-social-media-president/512405/

68 https://twitter.com/engineeringutsa?lang=en

69 Norrish, Mike "X helps Recovery of Lance Amstrong's Stolen
Bicycle," The Telegraph, February 2019 https://www.telegraph.
co.uk/sport/othersports/cycling/lancearmstrong/4696031/
Twitter-helps-recovery-of-Lance-Armstrongs-stolen-bicycle.html

70 Jarvis, Jeff "The X Flight (Well, Train)" Buzzmachine,
April 2009 https://buzzmachine.com/2009/04/29/
the-twitter-flight-well-train/

71 X Blog, https://marketing.twitter.com/na/en/success-stories/
how-heinz-harnessed-the-power-of-twitter-and-got-one-billion-
impressions

72 X Blog, https://developer.twitter.com/en/case-studies/dots.html

73 OmniCore Agency, "X by the Numbers: Stats, Demographics &
Fun Facts" September 2019
https://www.omnicoreagency.com/twitter-statistics/

74 https://blog.hjmt.com/2019/02/07/
our-ceo-interviewed-on-cbs-tv-as-expert-in-social-media/

75 Yelp Blog, https://www.yelp.com/factsheet

76 Davis, Joshua "The Secret World of LonelyGirl" Wired,
December 2006 https://www.wired.com/2006/12/lonelygirl/

77 Chi, Clifford, "2019 YouTube Demographics [New Data]"
Hubspot Blog, https://blog.hubspot.com/marketing/
youtube-demographics

78 Carter, Rebekah "Social Media Contests in 2018: Do They Still
Work?" Sprout Social December 2017 https://sproutsocial.com/
insights/social-media-contests/

79 "The State of Multimedia Press Releases" Cision January 2016 https://www.prnewswire.com/blog/2016/the-state-of-multimedia-in-press-releases-study-and-infographic.html

80 Andrew, Scottie and Ries, Brian "Long Before Ellen & Kim, There Was Robert Cornelius. He took the World's First Selfie Nearly 180 Years Ago," CNN June 2019 https://www.cnn.com/2019/06/21/us/national-selfie-day-first-selfie-trnd/index.html?no-st=1569348738

81 Andersen, Margaret "The Selfie as We Know it is Dead," Wired April 2018 https://www.wired.com/story/life-death-of-selfie/

82 Brown, Dalvin "Perfect Selfies are All Over Facebook, Instagram and Snapchat. They are Killing Us." USA Today, June 2019 https://www.usatoday.com/story/tech/2019/05/22/why-you-take-selfies-and-how-its-dangerous/3691366002/

83 Clement, J. "Share of US Adults Who Have Taken a Selfie 2018 By Age Group" Statista November 2018 https://www.statista.com/statistics/304861/us-adults-shared-selfie-generation/

84 Cohen, David "Selfies, Narcisson, and Social Media" AdWeek January 2016 https://www.adweek.com/digital/rawhide-selfies-infographic/

85 Winn, Ross "2019 Podcast Stats and Facts (New Research from June 2019)" PodcastInsights.com June 2019 https://www.podcastinsights.com/podcast-statistics/

86 Leadem, Rose "The Growth of Podcasts and Why it Matters" Entrepreneur Magazine December 2017 https://www.entrepreneur.com/article/306174

87 Chi, Clifford "Know in 2019" Hubspot Blog March 2019 https://blog.hubspot.com/marketing/youtube-stats

88 http://www.hjmtmedia.com

89 Stone, Bob and Jacobs, Ron "Direct Marketing Methods" December 2007 https://www.amazon.com/Successful-Direct-Marketing-Methods-Stone/dp/0071458298

90 Henneke, "37 Tips for Writing Emails that Get Opened, Read, and Get Clicked," CopyBlogger.com August 2013 https://www.copyblogger.com/37-email-marketing-tips/

91 AP, "Burger King Unveils Whopper Scented Cologne," November 2016 - https://www.foxnews.com/food-drink/burger-king-unveils-whopper-scented-cologne

92 ALS Website - http://www.alsa.org/fight-als/ice-bucket-challenge.html

93 Enberg, Jasmine "Digital Ad Spending 2019" eMarketer, March 2019 https://www.emarketer.com/content/global-digital-ad-spending-2019

94 https://shortyawards.com/8th/crossroads-community-street-fare-social-campaign-3

95 https://shortyawards.com/8th/love-has-no-labels-2

96 Hootsuite Blog, "How to Write a Social Media Policy for Your Company" July 2019 https://blog.hootsuite.com/social-media-policy-for-employees/

97 Dimock, Michael, "An update on our research into trust, facts and democracy" June 2019 Pew Research Study https://www.pewresearch.org/2019/06/05/an-update-on-our-research-into-trust-facts-and-democracy/

98 Newberry, Christine, "130+ Social Media Statistics that Matter to Marketers in 2019" Hootsuite Blog, March 2019 https://blog.hootsuite.com/social-media-statistics-for-social-media-managers/

99 Hootsuite Blog, "41 Facebook Stats that Matter to Marketers in 2019" November 2018 https://blog.hootsuite.com/facebook-statistics/

100 Lui, Shanhong "Market share of wearables unit shipments worldwide by vendor from 1Q'14 to 1Q'19" Statista, September 2019 https://www.statista.com/statistics/435944/quarterly-wearables-shipments-worldwide-market-share-by-vendor/

101 Hardwick, Tim, "Apple Watch Leads in Rapidly Growing Smartwatch Market, Report Says," MacRumors, February 2019 https://www.macrumors.com/2019/02/13/apple-watch-popularity-2018-smartwatch-market/

102 https://analytics.google.com/analytics/academy/course/8

103 https://www.searchenginejournal.com/google-analytics-4-vs-universal-analytics/385484/

* * *

Printed in the United States
by Baker & Taylor Publisher Services